Essential Tips
for Organizing
Conferences & Events

Essential Tips
for Organizing
Conferences & Events

Fiona Campbell,
Alison Robinson,
Sally Brown and
Phil Race

RoutledgeFalmer
Taylor & Francis Group

LONDON AND NEW YORK

First published in Great Britain and the United States in 2003 by RoutledgeFalmer

2 Park Square, Milton Park,   270 Madison Ave,
Abingdon, Oxon, OX14 4RN   New York NY 10016

Transferred to Digital Printing 2006

www.routledge.com
© Fiona Campbell, Alison Robinson, Sally Brown and Phil Race, 2003

The right of Fiona Campbell, Alison Robinson, Sally Brown and Phil Race to be identified as the authors of this work has been asserted by them in accordance with the Copyright, Designs and Patents Act 1988.

ISBN 0 7494 4039 2

British Library Cataloguing in Publication Data

A CIP record for this book is available from the British Library.

Library of Congress Cataloging-in-Publication Data
Essential tips for organizing conferences and events / Fiona Campbell
... [et al.].
    p. cm.
Includes bibliographical references (p.) and index.
  ISBN 0-7494-4039-2
  1. Special events–Planning. 2. Congresses and
conventions–Planning. I. Campbell, Fiona Louise, 1954–
  GT3405.E87 2003
  394.2′068–dc21
                                2003008164

Typeset by JS Typesetting Ltd, Wellingborough, Northants

Publisher's Note
The publisher has gone to great lengths to ensure the quality of this reprint but points out that some imperfections in the original may be apparent

Contents

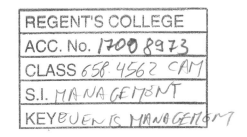

Preface

Like most things, learning to organize conferences and events is something that is best achieved by doing it. It is an experiential process. In particular, we have learnt through all the mistakes we have made in the conferences we have organized over many years – and perhaps even more from all the things that have gone wrong at the conferences and events we have attended as delegates throughout our careers. We have also learnt from the triumphs. The problem is that getting an event wrong is a very public affair, and does not always lead to opportunities to do it all better next time! This book is our attempt to help you to avoid making countless mistakes, and to allow you to benefit from the experience we have gained in organizing events.

There is no getting away from the fact that putting together a really good conference or event is hard work. There are all sorts of things to think about at the same time. There are several different timescales going on simultaneously. Above all, there can be the business of getting very different people to interact smoothly, happily and successfully – and that's just the conference team, let alone the delegates!

We have observed how many perfectly normal people like ourselves suddenly change when they become delegates. They become affected by a mysterious complaint which strikes as soon as they enter a conference venue. We have named it CADS: conference acquired dependency syndrome. There is more about this malady (and how to respond to people who have caught it) later in the book.

The most complex events to organize are major residential conferences, so we have devoted much of this book to considering this scale of event. However, the vast majority of the organizational aspects associated with conferences also apply to much smaller events, including half-day and one-day events, and indeed even shorter events such as public lectures, awards ceremonies, and after-dinner speeches.

All sorts of funded projects nowadays have dissemination events of one kind or another built in as part of their 'deliverables'. This means that an increasing number of people quite suddenly find themselves charged with the responsibility for putting on such events, sometimes at quite short notice, and often without having much experience in organizing such things. We hope that this book will bridge the gap between experienced conference organizers, and all the other people who find themselves plunged into the business at the deep end.

We have tried to make the suggestions we offer in this book practical, realistic and helpful. We have included a lot of detail where we think it will help. We have also opened up the agenda by including a section on 'Resources' which aims to be a starting point for some of the paperwork and administration in which you will doubtless find yourself immersed if you are organizing a conference, or even a much shorter event. We have also included a section of illustrative 'Templates' based on actual documentation that has been developed by very experienced conference organizers, so that you can tap in to their experience, rather than start from scratch in organizing your own events. These are designed to be used dynamically, and for you to pinch our best ideas and improve upon them.

We hope you will also enjoy one further dimension of this book, based on learning by getting things wrong – some case-study stories. We have tried to unpack some of the things that have been learnt from these.

Finally, we wish you luck as you go ahead organizing your own conferences and events. However carefully you plan these, some luck continues to be really useful – not least when it comes to the weather, if your event is to be held in a climate similar to that with which the UK is blessed.

Acknowledgements

We are grateful to all the colleagues with whom we have worked on countless conferences we have helped to organize, and to the even greater number of people whose conferences we have participated in over the years. All conferences should be learning experiences, not least about organizing conferences.

We are grateful to Brin Bowen and Phil Rodgers, two very experienced event managers, who gave us numerous additional suggestions towards the final stages of this book. We would also particularly like to thank Deb Chapman, who is a meticulous and fiercely constructive critic of our work, and has helped to make it a much better book.

This book is dedicated to the memory of Judy Yelland, a lovely, warm, dynamic person, who would have been delighted to see it in print.

1 Initiating the event: early decisions

Whether you are putting together your plans for a full-scale residential conference, or for a much shorter, sharper event, there is a lot of work involved! To keep you going when the going gets tough, you need good reasons to bother.

In this brief section, we have started with the overall question 'Why?' The remaining two elements of this section address the question 'What?', in the respective contexts of what will the event be about, and what will delegates get out it.

Our comments and suggestions in this section are of course expanded on considerably throughout much of the rest of this book, but we thought it best to start you thinking first about the global 'Why?' and 'What?' questions at the outset.

Why are you planning a conference or event?

Whether you are planning a residential conference running for several days, or a half-day training event, it takes a lot more time and energy to plan it all than just the time taken for it to run. It is not unusual for planning and organizing a big conference to take up several months of several people's time. Nor is it unusual for them to be busy people with all sorts of other things to attend to all through this time. It is therefore worth stepping back from the overall idea of planning a conference, and making sure that this is really what you want to do. The following questions and suggestions may help you to clear your mind, and decide why you're going to go ahead and organize a conference – or indeed not!

- **What are your objectives for the event?** What purposes will it serve you? In other words, what's in it for you if it goes really well? Promotion? Making an impact? Getting better known in your field? Public acclaim? Pleasing your boss? Just the satisfaction of having done it all and made it work? Some combination of several of these?

- **What's the risk for you?** What would be the worst-case scenario for you personally if the conference didn't work? Would any blame come firmly back to you?
- **Who will benefit from the conference?** Will it be the institution or venue at which the conference will take place, the organizing association, the participants themselves, the organizing team, sponsors if you happen to use them, or some combination of several of these possible beneficiaries? It is important to identify how each stakeholder is likely to benefit from the event.
- **What's in it for the host institution or the conference venue?** Is it likely that there will be a profit from the event? Will this be substantial? If the event is being hosted by an institution such as a university or college, is a profit expected by the host institution? Are other benefits more important to the institution, perhaps for example publicity? Would a loss be accepted if the event did not really take off?
- **What's in it for the members of the organizing team?** Will it bring them fame and fortune? Will it be a really useful professional development experience for them? Will it bring them job satisfaction and security? Will it open up new avenues? Will it bring them new important contacts and networking opportunities?
- **What's in it for the key presenters?** Will this be an important and timely opportunity for them to share their expertise? Will the conference open up to them important new channels of communication with others in their field? Will it allow them to gain recognition of their work? Will it lead to the successful publication of their work in reputable and esteemed formats?
- **What's in it for the delegates themselves?** What difference will the conference make to those who attend? What are they going to take away with them, in terms of knowledge, experience, skills and changed attitudes?
- **Does it really need to be a *conference* to meet the various needs of the various stakeholders?** In other words, do people need to be physically in the one place at the same time to achieve the objectives? Could your objectives be better served with an alternative mechanism? Perhaps a series of two-hour workshops, a team-building course, an on-line discussion forum, a self-instructional guide in printed or electronic form might be more appropriate?

Choosing themes

Getting the right people to a conference or training event depends substantially on making the event seem relevant, interesting and attractive for them. The following set of questions and suggestions should help you to make the crucial decisions about what exactly your conference will be seen to be about.

- **Will your topic remain topical?** Look at what is topical at the present time. Although some topics may have gone out of fashion only months later, most topical themes remain of interest for at least some time. Besides, even if perceptions about the theme may have changed by the time you actually run the conference, you will need to be attracting participants some time earlier than this. In any case, it is not difficult to continue to fine-tune exactly how the conference will address the themes all the way along the line to the event itself, and respond to emerging or changing views about the theme.

- **Are you and the planning team equipped with knowledge regarding national, institutional or local priorities?** Do you keep up to date by attending relevant events and following any national debate around the topic? If not, you should, and you should definitely make sure your team does include individuals who do.

- **Do you know your competition?** While you certainly won't want to run an identical event, it is likely that there will be similarities in the content and themes of corresponding events, if they relate to current priorities. Ensure that your event is complimentary rather than in competition. The number of potential delegates is finite, and you will both end up with low participation rates if events are too similar.

- **If it's a short, sharp event, don't make the theme too broad.** Your main aim should be to plan the advertising of the agenda for the event so that everyone who turns up for it will get at least some of what they are looking for from it.

- **Are there current hot issues or topical topics which you want to address?** Perhaps these have arisen as a result of changes in market forces, developments on the international scene or the creation of a new initiative or product?

- **What are the pressing interests and concerns of your target group?** What is it your people really want to do? Can this be turned into a conference theme?

- **Have there been national developments in the field?** Is there an obvious national agenda to be addressed? For example, has new legislation been issued which people will need to find out about and discuss? Are there funding body imperatives? Have new government initiatives been unveiled?

- **Is it likely to be something peculiar to your own organization?** Are there organizational priorities to agree on? Is an organization-based perspective required? Do the staff need upskilling in a particular area? Is there a new concept or initiative of relevance to your local group? Are there partnerships that require forging or opportunities to be created to facilitate the sharing of good practice?

- **Have more than one theme for a major event.** Often the most valuable products of a conference arise from different constituencies of delegates interacting with each other. If the agenda is too narrow, you may only attract people whose particular interest coincides exactly with this agenda.

- **Don't have too many themes.** If the conference themes appear to be too broad and varied, members of your target audiences are likely to think, 'Well, parts of this look relevant to me, but there's an awful lot that isn't directly useful to me,' and decide not to attend.

- **Don't expect to attract everyone in your target audiences.** Any conference will only attract a proportion of the target audience. Sometimes some of the most relevant potential delegates will simply not be able to attend through prior commitments, or for all sorts of other reasons.
- **Think ahead to strands.** For a major conference, it is normal to have parallel sessions, and to arrange these so that parallel strands follow through particular themes through the conference. These strands can be developed from the original advertised themes.
- **Don't expect all envisaged strands to become a reality.** When conference publicity identifies a number of intended strands, it is normal for one or two of these to attract the greatest interest and large numbers of contributions, and for what seemed to be equally viable strands to turn out to be non-starters. It is also normal for some better ways of dividing the conference into strands to become apparent when the nature and direction of most of the contributions become clearer, near to the event.

Intended conference outcomes

In education and training, it is normal to describe the curriculum in terms of what is intended to be achieved. This is often done in terms of 'objectives', or 'intended learning outcomes' or 'intended training outcomes'. One way or another, these boil down to spelling out in advance what people who participate should achieve by the end of the event. It can be really useful to spell out the agenda of a conference or training event in similar ways, so that people making up their minds about whether to take part can get a better idea of what's in it for them if they attend – or indeed what they may miss out on if they don't attend.

- **Think of what people are likely to *want* to get out of the event.** What will get them to sign up for the event in the first place? How will participation in the event match their interests and aspirations?
- **Think of what people may *need* to get out of the event.** What are their problems? What may they gain at the event to address these problems? What kinds of solutions to these problems may the event help them to identify?
- **Don't set out too many intended conference outcomes.** For a big event, the intended outcomes could run into pages. Pick out only the intended outcomes that are likely to be highest on intended participants' shopping lists.
- **Beware of stating things that intended participants may already have achieved.** If the event looks as though it won't take them any further, they are unlikely to enrol for it. Build in to the wording of each of the intended outcomes some feeling of how they will take their existing achievements further or deeper.

- **Aim to make the intended outcomes tangible and achievable.** Avoid bland wording such as 'understand', 'know' or 'appreciate'. Focus instead on what participants will be able to do with their increased understanding, knowledge or appreciation by the end of the event.
- **Link the intended outcomes demonstrably to the themes of the event.** For example, have one or two intended outcomes linked to each theme.
- **Use the intended outcomes to spell out exactly what the themes are likely to mean in practice for those who participate in the event.** The wording of a theme may only tell intending delegates something about the content of the event; the intended outcomes can add vital detail about what exactly intending delegates may hope to achieve in relation to each theme.
- **Make the intended outcomes link well to being present and participating at the event.** This can be done quite explicitly, for example by phrasing them along the lines, 'After participating in this conference, and taking part in the discussions, brainstorming sessions, and workshop tasks, you should be better able to:
  - put into practice. . .
  - develop workable tactics to. . .
  - work towards achieving. . .
- **Test out your ideas of intended conference outcomes with typical intended participants.** For example, ask them to jot down their thoughts in answer to 'What three things would you particularly like the planned conference to do for you?' and see what the most common threads turn out to be. This can also help you to identify further themes – or indeed to find out which of the current themes in your draft planning don't actually lead directly enough into any intended outcomes for delegates.

2 Choosing the right type of event

What is the right type of event? This depends mainly on the purpose of your event, as well as the size, duration, history, and other circumstances surrounding your planning and implementation of the event.

We start this section with a table illustrating some of the similarities and differences between a range of different kinds of event. However, these are not mutually exclusive, as for example it is quite common to have a 'launch' event within a residential conference, and even more common to have a formal dinner and after-dinner speech. But launch events and dinners with speakers can be free-standing events in their own right too.

We therefore continue this section with the question, 'What sort of event are you planning?' and some comments and suggestions to help you to think deeper into your overall rationale. We continue by posing the question, 'When is a conference the best choice?' to help you think through the basis on which you may choose a conference as the most suitable format for your event.

We complete this section of the book by looking individually at one-day events, half-day events, awards ceremonies and launch events. There are of course similarities and differences between all of these possibilities, and it is often the case that a longer event such as a conference may also include one or more of these.

What sort of event are you planning?

The suggestions and discussions in this book extend to several kinds of event, for example international conferences, national and internal conferences, launch and dissemination events, and so on. Different kinds of event serve different purposes. It's important to choose the right kind of event for the purposes you are aiming to achieve. Some things lend themselves to full-scale international conferences; other purposes are best served by shorter, sharper local gatherings. It is useful to make wise and informed choices regarding the sort of event that will best meet your particular requirements and contexts. The following questions and suggestions may help you to decide which kind of event will be most suitable for your purposes.

Table 2.1 *Choosing your event format*

Type of event	Sample reasons for choosing this type of event	Audience possibilities	Scope	Reasonable planning lead time	Organizational workload	Use for Continuing Professional Development
Residential conference: 1 week or more	Bring together wide audience for concentrated period of work and pleasure	International or national, or occasionally organizational	Wide-ranging, complex, multiple themes, chance to work in breadth and depth	18 months	High	Usually
Residential conference: 2-3 days	Wide audience of people who can't meet otherwise, and who can't spend too many days away from base	International or national, or regional		18 months	High	Usually
One-day event	Tight focus on a single area theme or discipline	National or regional	Relatively specific theme or focus	6 months	Medium	Often
Half-day event or training workshop	Relatively cheap event for busy people; restricted area or topic	Local, or internal or institutional	Specific theme or focus	6 months	Medium	Often
Expert seminar	Bring together a group of experts to share knowledge and experience	Invited experts	Quite specific, perhaps a single issue	6 months	Medium	Often
Public lecture	Focus on a key specialist or special topic	All comers	Various	3 months	Low	Sometimes
Invited lecture, eg 'endowed' or 'memorial' lecture	Showcase a particular speaker to a selected audience	Limited known audience	Various, often scholarly or expert	3 months	Low	Sometimes
Symposium or debate	Hear a range of views on a particular topic or theme	Varied. Can overlap with conferences or other events	Scholarly event, emphasising discussion	6–12 months	Medium or high	Often
Launch event	Introduce a topic, organization, or product	Target audience for product, organization or a particular development	Various	6–12 months	High	Rarely
Award event	Celebrate achievements or successes	Nominees, winners, VIPs and guests	Focus on winners	6–9 months	High	Sometimes
Annual General Meeting	Fulfil a statutory requirement of a charitable or voluntary body	Members and officers	Administrative, planning, development	12 months	Medium	Not relevant
Dinner and after-dinner speech	Organizational or group celebration	Organization members and guests	Celebration, entertainment, bonding	6 months	Medium	Not relevant

- **Do you intend to bring together an international group to discuss and take forward a particular theme?** In this case, you are probably working towards organizing a fully-fledged international residential conference.
- **Is the conference part of a series?** In this case, you will need to take due account of how recent conferences in the series have developed over the last few years. In such cases it is well worthwhile for you, and other key members of your organizing team, to have attended the last two or three in the series. If it's a big conference, it will be even better if your team can attend the conference before yours *en masse*, and shadow the team that is running it in the venue concerned.
- **Is the target audience well defined?** Do you want to bring together a group of staff from different agencies, organizations and institutions to address particular themes? If so, a national residential conference may be suitable. This is the most usual format of annual conferences organized by professional associations.
- **Is the need or purpose more localized?** For example, does the purpose relate principally to a particular group of staff within a particular region? Purposes could include reaching a set of decisions or action planning to tackle a certain issue. If so, your event is most likely to be a one-day regional conference or training event.
- **Are you planning to launch something?** Perhaps a new association, a new funding stream, a new national or local initiative, or a new concept? If so, a national one-day event could be suitable, with most or many people travelling some distance to attend.
- **Do you wish to disseminate information and ideas from a funded project or a new initiative?** Again a one-day national or regional event may be the best way to meet your needs. There may well be at least some dissemination funding already built into the project, some of which could go towards the costs of planning and running a conference or event.
- **Is your event focused on one institution or organization?** If so a one-day in-house event may be the most useful format (although you may choose not to hold the event on-site). Events of this kind could include a conference run for staff of a particular organization (usually with external inputs), which aims to agree an organizational perspective on a particular issue, or to enhance staff awareness and abilities in a specific area.
- **How big will your event be?** How many participants do you anticipate? Be realistic and use as a guide numbers who have attended similar events – although be aware that location, timing, and factors about the timeliness of the topic may all affect expected numbers. Many of these factors are covered in other parts of this book.

When is a conference the best choice?

Why would you want to choose to have a *conference*? When deciding what kind of an event to have, you are likely to want to think through the pros and cons of having a conference, rather than a different kind of event. The following sets of tips are designed to help you make this decision. Here we are using the term 'conference' to mean a substantial event at which delegates can hear a range of keynote and other speakers, participate in discussions and workshops, and review exhibitions and displays.

Conferences can be suitable for:

- **Enabling opportunities for delegates to hear from established and highly regarded experts in the field.** It can be extremely stimulating to hear, direct from the 'horse's mouth', what is the current state of play in a particular field. It can also make concepts and ideas that are reasonably familiar come to life when heard direct from the lips of a recognized authority.
- **Offering opportunities for delegates to network with a wide range of people who share with them an area of interest.** Many delegates indicate in their feedback from conferences that the most useful aspect of the event has been talking through ideas with other fellow participants and finding out how they are interpreting ideas and data in contiguous fields. Although electronic communication is now ubiquitous, there is no substitute for face-to-face meetings, where seemingly tangential and perhaps inconsequential encounters can sometimes suddenly appear relevant and exciting.
- **Offering the organizers the chance to showcase particular areas of work.** This may include projects that are nearing their conclusion, or research work that merits wider attention, or well-regarded small-scale work that has not yet impacted highly on the community at large.
- **Enabling participants to bounce ideas off other interested parties and get feedback on work in progress.** Publishing ideas in print or electronically establishes and fixes your work in the intellectual domain, but when work is incomplete, discussing it at a conference can be extremely helpful both to the originator and to those who provide commentary.
- **Offering fast opportunities to establish ideas in a context.** A conference can provide opportunities for work to be disseminated more quickly than paper publication sometimes allows. Articles in journals are often written months or years before they are in press, so conferences can offer immediate chances for the work to be placed in the public domain.
- **Providing a space away from their normal environment for delegates to concentrate on important and topical subjects.** The daily life of academia or business often fails to provide opportunities for 'blue skies' thinking, digestion and consolidation, but the atmosphere at a well-run conference can enable a level of analysis that may not be possible in everyday life.

- **Providing informal and social opportunities for members of a learning community to interact.** It is often the informal, accidental, casual encounters between colleagues talking in the lunch queue or on the bus *en route* to the conference social events that can be the most productive for delegates. A well-run conference can be a highly enjoyable place to learn, and one in which the boundaries between work and pleasure often break down to beneficial effect.
- **Offering the chance for delegates to broaden perspectives.** In the case of international conferences particularly, such occasions provide delegates with the opportunity to travel, share their views with people from different cultures and nations, and develop new perspectives on topics of high interest and relevance to them.
- **For the organizers, conferences may provide opportunities for income generation.** This should not be assumed always to be the case, however, since there is a lot of competition for conference income and the only conferences to make a profit are those where budgetary planning is meticulous, where contingencies have been planned for in advance and where realistic assumptions have been made at the outset. There is also an element of luck around choosing the topics, managing to find the best speakers available and hitting the right timing for the subject matter.

One-day events

One-day events seem to be becoming ever more popular. This is partly because busy professional people may find it easier to find a single day they can squeeze out of their diaries, when it would not have been possible to be away for even two days. However, the skills you need to organize a successful, well-attended one-day event are no less than for a much bigger event. Many of the tips elsewhere in this book continue to apply, but the following additional guidance may help you on your way to planning a good one-day event.

- **Don't underestimate the size of the organizational task.** Organizing a one-day event needs as careful planning as organizing a full conference, so refer to the tips elsewhere about planning, signage, registration, costing and so on. You need to be on top of all the separate steps for successful event organization, even though the event is on a smaller scale than a full conference.
- **Consider having an event manager on duty throughout the day.** While at a one-day event you may not need a fully staffed registration point or reception desk all day, it can be useful to have one non-participating person on hand, to deal with equipment suppliers, breakdowns, messages for delegates, enquiries, checking that refreshments are available where and

when they should be, and all the sorts of things that can need sorting out even in a relatively small gathering of people. Professional event managers find no difficulty in keeping themselves suitably occupied during the few periods of a one-day event when no one needs their help.

- **What can the venue provide?** If you are arranging a one-day event in a hotel, for example, it's worth finding out what it can do for you, and how much it may cost. For example, can it provide photocopying at short notice, including making overhead transparencies? It is worth also checking out whether there may be a convenient photocopying and printing shop within five minutes' walk, where the prices may be much lower and the quality much better.

- **Anticipate mobility needs.** Commercial venues such as hotels usually have disabled toilet facilities, but some rooms may only be accessible by stairs, especially break-out or syndicate rooms.

- **Be particularly careful in your specification of the target audience.** A one-day event is likely to be much more specific and focused than a residential conference. It is therefore critical that the 'right' people choose to attend – and indeed that the 'wrong' people don't! Your publicity material needs to have clear statements following on from a starter along the lines, 'This event is intended for people such as. . .', or 'This event will be useful for you if you are. . .' and so on.

- **Consider the extent to which you are prepared to help with residential arrangements.** Even with one-day events, some delegates may wish to stay over the night before or after (or both). By all means see if you can negotiate a cheap rate with a local hotel and/or provide information for delegates about local accommodation, but be aware that you could double your administration load if you get involved with taking bookings for hotel accommodation.

- **Plan the shape of the day with the delegates' experience in mind.** Plan the programme by thinking about what the delegates are likely to want, rather than what you want to tell them. Where possible, it is often helpful to have a couple of people on the planning team who represent your target audience.

- **Make your timetable realistic.** One of the dangers with one-day events is that of cramming too much into them. It is tempting to try to get half a dozen inputs into a one-day event, but it is often better to have fewer inputs and more opportunities for delegates to discuss the material. Over-filling the day often means that individual elements of the day tend to overrun, and this can cascade as the day continues, leading to unsatisfactory 'squeezing' of the elements planned for later in the day. In any case, very few people can give their full attention to a series of presentations all day long without interruption.

- **Plan your start time carefully.** Work out how many of your delegates are likely to be travelling from some distance to the venue on the day, and decide what would be a realistic start time for them. It can be useful to consult rail or air timetables for the main centres your delegates could be travelling from, and even to suggest, in your event publicity or joining instructions, train times or flights that would get them comfortably to the venue by the start time.

- **Try to ensure that all delegates arrive in time for the start of the event.** It can be useful to make sure that the first main session will be seen as a really important, useful element of the day by most who will be attending. This more than anything else is likely to spur them to make their travel arrangements to arrive promptly.

- **Plan your finish time appropriately.** It is well known that 4 pm on a Friday is likely to be too late for many delegates. When most delegates will be travelling some distance after the event, it is useful to think about train or flight times, and local knowledge about rush-hour congestion. Providing a coach to the main station at 4.30 in time for a 5 pm train can ensure that delegates don't begin slipping away in taxis from much earlier than 4.30, for example.

- **Try to keep your delegates there till the end.** It can help if you save something important for the last element of the programme. If it is just a routine report-back from group tasks, many delegates may not stay for it. A short but important plenary keynote is often the most successful tactic in keeping delegates till the end. In any case, it is much better for everyone's overall impression of the day if a one-day event ends with a bang rather than fizzles out.

- **Work out your intended outcomes for the event.** With short events, it becomes even more crucial that delegates get what they expect from the event, and if your publicity misleads them, they will not be pleased (to say the least). Therefore work out up to half a dozen (but no more) intended outcomes for them, so they can make a realistic decision about whether to book your event.

- **Make your intended outcomes realistic.** In a short event, it is important that you don't promise what you can't deliver. It is fine to end up delivering more than you spelt out in the intended outcomes publicity, but avoid the risk of the event not being able to cover all that you promised.

- **Try to plan in variety.** Sitting on one seat for one presentation after another soon causes delegates to lose interest – and to lose patience. A change of room can be refreshing, but a change of activity may be even better. It can be helpful to balance a one-day programme between keynotes, plenary discussions, parallel sessions, and choices from a workshop menu.

- **Don't hurry the breaks.** Thirty-minute coffee breaks tend to work much better than attempted 15-minute breaks, which invariably lead to a slack start to the ensuing part of the day's programme. At a one-day event, opportunities for socializing are very limited, so people who have the need to have informal meetings and catch up with each other may be tempted to miss sessions if you don't provide some space in the day for interactions. Additionally, for one-day events you may have present people who have made very early starts to be there at the beginning of the day and who are anticipating long journeys home, so they are likely to get exhausted.

- **Don't skimp on refreshments.** For those with early starts, the tea or coffee on arrival is an essential rather than a luxury. An early refreshment period also provides 'catch-up time' for those who have experienced travel difficulties.
- **However, few people usually stay for the final cup of tea at the very end of the day.** They are often rushing for trains/planes or to miss the rush-hour traffic. While some may welcome a last cuppa, cut numbers down if you are ordering catering for a final refreshment period. In practice, the people who will continue for this last phase of a one-day event are those who have no particular need to depart yet, or who are waiting around in any case for later travel times or connections.
- **Don't forget to seek feedback.** Delegates at major conferences are usually relatively willing to provide feedback, as their feedback will shape the next conference, and so on. At one-day events, there may not be any similar perceived benefit for delegates. And because of the shorter timescale, it can be harder actually to get delegates at a one-day event to fill out question-naires, so you might consider having some sort of prize draw associated with the feedback process, or make your questionnaire particularly short, sharp and interesting to complete (there's a challenge!).
- **Learn from feedback.** Despite the difficulty of getting feedback, if you are running a series of one-day events, you can learn a great deal along the series, and continue to fine-tune the formats, timings and processes to suit an ever greater proportion of those who attend.

You just can't win them all!

What happened?

Maybe it was the timing (early November) or maybe it was the topic (although it had recruited really well previously), and the presenter was well known and highly regarded. Whatever the cause, hardly anyone had signed up for the one-day workshop a couple of days before it was to run.

The organizers considered cancelling it, but the date for doing so without penalty had passed and they felt that there might be bad PR fall-out in letting down those paying participants who had booked. The facilitator was anxious, though, because the workshop had been designed to be very interactive and she needed at least 12 people present to make the group exercises work properly.

Then one of the organizing team had a brainwave. The topic was one that was likely to be beneficial for a number of the organization's own staff, and it was also agreed that some of those on the administration side who had responsibility for making other events work would learn a lot from watching one in action, even if the subject wasn't central to their roles. In addition, it would be better to let the 'home' staff have a nice lunch in a local hotel rather than let meals that had to be paid for go to waste.

So they went ahead, and all was going well until early afternoon when the presenter stepped outside the hotel for a breath of air when the participants were on task. The venue was 200 yards from a river which was rapidly rising to its highest level for 400 years. As the water came within 10 yards of the hotel, it was felt necessary immediately to halt the workshop and send everyone home before it was too late.

Learning points

- When running one-day workshops, it is best not to confirm finally a booking with the venue until you have recruited enough participants at least to break even.
- Ideally, find out in advance from venues if they would be prepared to transfer a booking to a later date even when you have confirmed, if numbers are much lower than expected. That way you might still be able to cancel without losing your deposit.
- Think well in advance about foreseeable contingencies (like low numbers booking when the facilitator needs a minimum number to make a critical mass) and if possible insure against them.
- Try to think laterally when problems are seemingly insoluble. And accept there are just some things that you cannot anticipate!

Half-day events

Many of the suggestions throughout this book continue to apply to organizing and running events that only last for part of one day. In particular, most of the suggestions on one-day events are still relevant. However, some additional tips for half-day events are offered below.

- **Think carefully about your kick-off time.** If it is an in-house event, those attending may be already on-site, and your choices of starting time are wider. But if they are all on-site at 9 am, starting at 10 am may not be a good idea, as some (sometimes many!) are likely to have got waylaid by dealing with e-mails, phone calls, urgent things that have just come up, and so on. If it is an event most people will be travelling to, an early morning start time could involve people in higher costs in terms of peak-hour train fares, and/or time wasted in rush-hour traffic. An 11 am start, with lunch at 12.30, and then sessions from 1.30 to 3.00 can be a good compromise for many travelling to half-day events.

- **Consider starting with lunch.** Where an afternoon event is a suitable option, starting with an optional lunch is one way of making sure that most of those attending will be there for the opening of the event. The disadvantage is that it is often difficult to get good estimates of the numbers who will actually arrive in time for lunch, so judging the quantity of catering is quite problematic.

- **Don't rule out evening events.** It is worth doing your market research, and finding out how many potential delegates would find an evening half-day event perfectly acceptable. For example, busy professional people may find it possible to escape from their normal work a little early, and be able to participate. Be careful not to end up discriminating against those with family commitments, such as picking up kids from school. At the same time, it can often be easier to find suitable, affordable facilities during evening time, for example teaching rooms in universities or colleges which would otherwise be empty. And car parking may be more widely available. It remains advisable to have some way of providing refreshments before the event, for those who have come away from work to reach it.

- **Be really careful about the publicity.** Especially when at least some people may be spending several hours travelling to – and from – a half-day event, if the event does not live up to their expectations they can be really annoyed. This means being clear about how you describe your target audience, joining instructions, intended outcomes of the event and so on. You may find it useful to look elsewhere in the book to the detailed suggestions offered to those running workshops at larger conferences, and fine-tune your event's rationale, outcomes and timetable accordingly.

- **Consider playing it again.** Sometimes it is worth having a half-day event run two or three times, perhaps at different times of the day, on different days of the week, and perhaps in different venues, so that potential participants have a choice. This is not usually an option where keynote presentations are involved – few keynoters are willing to give the same presentation more than once. Where the event is a dissemination event, however, the group providing it may find it worthwhile to reach more of their target audience by offering repeat events.

- **Draft your outline programme carefully.** Ideally, you want your delegates to be there right from the start of the event itself, so the programme needs to look as though it starts with something too important to miss. However, even with short events, it's often the case that at least some delegates are delayed, so try to make the really important opening element something that happens perhaps 15 minutes after the formal opening, so that everyone is likely to be there for this element.

Awards ceremonies

One of the specialist types of event you may wish to organize is an event at which institutional, regional, national or international awards are given. Obviously these are likely to be highly enjoyable for those who are receiving the awards, and you will therefore want to make sure that everything goes as smoothly as possible.

- **Consider carefully who gets invited.** At some awards ceremonies, all nominated or short-listed candidates are invited and the final list is only revealed at the last minute. At others, only the recipients and their guests are present, together with other invitees. There is more excitement at the former type of event, while the latter is likely to have a calmer, more celebratory atmosphere for all. As with other high profile events, you may wish to have an 'A' list of invitees and a list of reserves to fill gaps at tables if anyone drops out at the last minute.
- **Think carefully about the order of events.** You will need to have a clear running order so that everyone (including venue and catering staff, audio-visual personnel and guests) knows exactly what happens when.
- **Timing is all.** If you have a high-profile person presenting the awards, you are likely to have less control of your event's timing, as you are likely to have to fit in with their availability. Make sure that if the awards are, for example, after dinner, that you can be sure that the food will be served and cleared in time for the speeches to start. Allow time in your schedule for slippage if people are late or slow.
- **Decide who is in charge of keeping the event on time and on target.** An experienced Master or Mistress of Ceremonies with a good voice and charisma is invaluable, who can act as a 'ringmaster' to keep the show on the road and to improvise as necessary.
- **Have a contingency plan if things go wrong.** Make sure you know what you will do if any of the parties involved doesn't show up, and ideally have nominated stand-ins for key personnel for emergency use.
- **Get the catering right.** At an event like this, the food is not likely to be the main thing on people's minds, but it still needs to be appropriate, acceptable to people with all kinds of dietary needs and enjoyable. The award recipients will not thank you if the food they are served before they collect their awards is messy to eat!
- **Think about people with special needs.** Avoid the embarrassment of failing to make it easy for wheelchair users, or people with visual impairments, to go up and collect awards by planning for this in advance. Consider using signers for people with auditory difficulties.
- **Make sure you have time for a walk-through.** If the awards are yet to be announced, you obviously can't rehearse all of the likely recipients, but you

can have a walk-through by the other key participants, or by stand-ins if high-profile presenters cannot be there until the event itself.

- **Brief your award recipients well.** Let them know what will be expected of them, what the dress code of the event is, whether they will be expected to speak, who they will be meeting, and other key information.
- **Consider how best to keep the recipients' stress levels down.** Asking them to speak in response to an award at a large gathering can be nerve-wracking for some, although others would hate to miss the opportunity. For some, just walking up and collecting the award is almost more than they can take.
- **Go easy on the alcohol before the awards are given out.** It is inadvisable to enable your recipients to become too 'tired and emotional' before they accept their awards. Afterwards is a very different matter!
- **Make the route your award recipients take to the podium as simple as possible.** You may wish to use marshals to collect up the award winners, point them in the right direction and prompt them when to go up to collect their awards.
- **Think about what you will be giving your award winners to carry away.** If they have a certificate, you will need to be sure that you have a mechanism in place to ensure they get the right one. If you are giving them trophies, or other substantial items to carry, consider having these available after they have stepped off the podium.
- **Work out when you will take photographs.** You may not wish to interrupt the flow of your event by having a photo taken as each recipient goes up, but recipients will certainly want an individual record of the event, and high-profile presenters may not be willing to wait behind after the awards to have posed photos taken. Don't forget to brief photographers if you want group shots and general shots as well, and consider sending a member of staff round with the photographer to record names of people in shot.
- **Think about how you will manage audio-visual components.** Decide whether you will manage this yourself or use a specialist company for your event. If you are unsure what you want, ask a number of companies to quote for different kinds of presentation support (video, tape slide, music and so on) and use their expertise to help you make a decision in your price range. Live music feels celebratory and is flexible, but can be less predictable than pre-recorded music. Video often turns out to be an expensive alternative, but can have high impact.
- **Work out how you want the event to end.** Plan carefully for the dismantling of any set (display stands, staging, and so on – people whose business is event management call this the 'break-down' of the set) and for how you will tactfully usher your invitees out of the venue on time. Don't forget that most venues charge extra if you overstay your booked time, particularly at the end of an evening event, where they are likely to have to pay staff overtime if you run late.

Launch events

Some of the events you wish to organize may be to launch a project, a publication or a new organization. The planning and execution for such an event needs to be meticulous and flawless (at least to the delegates present), as you want to give as good an impression as possible of your new venture. A badly organized or attended launch will set you off to a poor start from which it may be difficult to recover, while a highly successful one can be the springboard for exciting new developments. Here are some questions you might want to ask yourself when organizing a launch.

- **How many people can you invite?** You need to consider your available budget carefully to make sure you can afford what you are doing. You will need to draw up a complete budget plan from the outset so you are clear about what you can and can't do.
- **What kind of event do you want?** Is it to be glitzy and glamorous, classy but restrained, or workmanlike and low key? Public sector or charitable organizations may get very poor press if they appear to be lavishly expending other people's money, but on the other hand, you want to put on a good show that will introduce your project, product or people in an appropriate manner.
- **What kind of venue do you want?** Your answer will of course depend on your responses to the questions above. If you go for a commercial venue like a hotel, a museum/art gallery or a conference centre, you are likely to get a very professional service but it will be expensive. Academic venues can be less expensive (but will not necessarily be so), but you may find you are doing more of the legwork yourself. It may be worth using an event management company to help you find the most appropriate venue.
- **Who do you want to be there?** Targeting your invitation list can be key to the success of your launch. Identify the people you ideally would like to attend, and aim high by targeting figures such as government ministers, national or international figures and media colleagues. You won't get many of these to most occasions, but you won't get any at all if you don't ask them.
- **What will the invitation list actually look like?** Who must you invite (such as sponsors, steering committee members, local dignitaries)? Who would really appreciate the invitation? Who is likely actually to be able to be there? You are trying to balance getting the largest numbers possible of the right kinds of people there, without creating too ambitious a list of people, not many of whom are likely to attend. You might also want to draw up a list of 'reserve invitees' who can be approached at shorter notice to attend, once some of your 'A' list have declined your invitation.

- **How can you identify your list of invitees?** What mailing lists can you access (with due reference to Data Protection Act) in order to draw up your invitation list? How much work do you need to do on the Web to identify your target invitees? Who can help you find the people you want to attend? How can you make sure you don't miss out anyone important?

- **How much of the work are you prepared to do yourself?** You can use event management or PR companies to run the whole event for you, or you can do it yourself. If the latter, do you have the resources within your own team, or do you need to hire in extra help? If so, make sure your budget reflects this. If the former, get really clear agreements about who is doing what and what you will be paying. It's very easy to run away with budgets in the heat of the moment.

- **What format do you want the event to have?** Try to avoid boring your invitees to death by having too many speeches. Advise your speakers to keep their inputs short and to the point. Focus as much as you can on what is being launched. If there is a key moment to the event, such as making live a Web site, cutting a ribbon or unveiling a plaque, make this central to the launch. Don't do it too early while people are still arriving, or too late when people have started to drift off. Make sure there is time for people to circulate and talk to one another.

- **Who will be in charge of making the event run to schedule?** Will you ask a high profile person to act as Master (or Mistress) of Ceremonies for the day? If so, this person will need careful briefing about the order of play and the tone you would like him or her to set.

- **What kind of equipment will you need?** Will you need to hire in public address facilities, or does the venue provide this? Do you need a data projector or other means of supporting your speakers? What about display boards?

- **Will you want photographs or a video of the event?** If so, do you need professional help? Build this into your budget if you want to have high-quality records of the event, and brief the personnel very carefully about the kind of images you want recorded (just headshots of the key presenters, or general crowd shots, or particular types of picture?).

- **What kind of catering will you offer?** A sit-down lunch may seem like a good idea but gives few opportunities for participant circulation. A buffet may be better if you want invitees to talk to one another. An afternoon tea is cost-effective if funds are short. Some kinds of event are unthinkable without offering alcohol, but at others it would be entirely inappropriate. If you do offer alcohol, make sure there are pleasant alternatives (for instance, at a champagne reception you will want to offer more than mineral water as an alternative) for those who do not drink.

- **How will you make the event feel like a celebration?** Will you be decorating the venue in some way? Will there be flowers? Do you want live music as background (this is often less expensive than you might think to arrange)?

- **How are you going to publicize the event?** Will you be aiming for press coverage? In this case you will need to invite and brief journalists well in advance so they can put your event into their diaries. Make sure you plan in time for writing and circulating press releases and for responding to press calls during the event. If it is a major launch, consider providing a press room at the venue to enable you to offer facilities for interviews with key participants. You may also consider preparing a 'press pack' of the information you most want to convey to journalists, or additional background that will help them write the story. You are more likely to get the story you want (or indeed any story rather than no story at all) if you make it easy for them by providing the right information.
- **How will you know who is there?** You will almost certainly need a reception desk so you can check who has arrived and who has not shown up. If you have key invitees you want to look after particularly well, your reception staff will need a photo sheet so they can identify your VIPs on arrival and point them out to the organizers. (You can often get photos of key figures from their Web sites.) Consider whether your event is the kind where asking people to wear badges will be appropriate.
- **What are you going to do if things go wrong?** As with all other events, it is important to have contingency plans, particularly if one of your top speakers is likely to be called away to more important business, as is often the unavoidable case with VIPs. If anyone in your event is 'mission-critical' you need to have an understudy in the wings ready to stand in at the last moment. It is a good idea to plan out some contingencies. For example, if you are launching a Web site, have it available in dummy form rather than rely on live network connections.
- **Think about security implications.** If you are relying on high-profile public or political figures to attend or speak at your event, you will need to think about security carefully. You may also need to consider enhanced security arrangements if you are launching a politically contentious product, concept, or alliance. Think about whether your venture might attract adverse attention from (for example) animal rights activists, anti-war campaigners or anti-capitalist protesters. Some activist groups can be only too willing to attract publicity by interrupting any high-profile event, especially where media presence is also likely to be there, and all the more so when a speaker or delegate is known to be a high-profile person.
- **Do you want to produce a pack of materials for invitees?** At some events it is really helpful to offer speaker biographies, texts of presentations, and information about the product, organization or project you are launching in the form of a presentation pack. At black tie dinners, this may be less helpful.
- **What follow-up work do you need to do?** You many wish to circulate to invitees and the press the texts of some or all of the inputs. You are also likely to want to follow up key contacts. Don't forget the courtesies of thanking people, both your speakers and those who have worked hard to make the event a success.

21

3 Choosing the right inputs for your event

The most successful conferences have a range of inputs which enable participants to be drawn into the content in different ways. Whether you are planning a full-scale conference, or a shorter focused event, you are likely to wish to have more than one kind of input. Different inputs enable participants to do different things. So what do you want your participants to do? To listen? To discuss? To work collaboratively? To share good practice? To gain practical skills? To network? To interact? To reach collective decisions? All of these? Some of these? Something else?

A range of inputs also means changes in pace, delivery and style which will stimulate participants and encourage them to engage with the conference themes. However the different types of input will have to reflect the conference aims, the nature of the theme, the available time for the event and the type of accommodation you are using. The following section outlines the most common kinds of input elements, and provides suggestions on how you can get the most out of each.

We start with 'keynotes', then follow through our analysis by addressing plenary sessions, workshops and presentations, discussion sessions, networking sessions, poster exhibitions and commercial exhibitions. These are, of course, not the only kinds of inputs that can make up an overall event, but we hope that the suggestions we have provided in this section will get you off to a good start if you are considering yet more kinds of input for your event.

Keynotes

However much planning you put into your event, however well you have done the costings, however brilliantly the organization of it runs, the event will not be regarded as a success if your keynote addresses, presentations, workshops and discussions are regarded by delegates as weak, insubstantial, uninteresting or lacking in appeal. The presenters you choose to give keynotes are critical to the success of the event. The presenters of keynotes will need to stimulate the participants, provide valuable information and set the tone for the event. But how can you find these paragons? And how can you ensure that they will meet your needs? The following tips are designed to help you ensure that the quality of the content of the event is as high as your organizational arrangements.

- **Think carefully why you are going to use keynotes.** Keynote presentations provide an opportunity for participants to learn from specialists in the field. A 'big name' can give credibility to the proceedings and is likely to promote attendance. Keynotes also help to cement the conference by encapsulating the conference agenda. They are useful at the start of a conference, to provide a common platform of knowledge which participants can debate.
- **Try for topical subjects, which have not become hackneyed.** People will book to attend an event on the strength of a single well-known, excellent speaker talking on an up-to-date hot topic, but it is difficult to plan this for events organized a long way ahead. Sound out people in the know for advice on what topics are on the horizon and which ones have been done to death.
- **Choose principal speakers carefully.** Will they be good enough? There are countless tales of terrible keynotes. The person who wrote the definitive book or article is not necessarily wonderful at putting the same message across to a large group face to face. If your conference or training event uses one or more keynote speakers, it is really important that you organize such elements thoroughly and in good time. An event can be lifted by a brilliant, charismatic speaker who enthuses and motivates the audience, and can equally be wrecked by one who is lacklustre, unoriginal or just plain boring. Never just book a published 'name' without checking that he or she can present as effectively in public as he or she writes.
- **Work carefully with personal assistants.** Often keynoters are busy people, and their PAs could be the people you deal with. In such cases, try to make sure that the keynoters themselves really do know exactly what they are being brought in to talk about. For example, one national figure was advertised to be talking on 'Middle schools', but actually turned up to speak on 'Middle years in secondary schools', as his PA did not realize there was a difference.
- **Get some opinions from other people.** Ideally, sound out two or three people you respect who have heard your main speakers elsewhere, and check that they will give you what you want. Have you or a member of the planning team come across possible keynotes at conferences you have attended? Accept recommendations for keynote speakers only from those who have witnessed the individual's performance as a speaker elsewhere, to ensure their style of delivery suits your event. Use all possible sources of information to find out which keynote speakers will be best for your particular event.
- **Clarify your expectations at the outset.** If you want a straightforward speech with questions at the end, specify this. If you want something more inter-active, then brief accordingly. If it is not acceptable to your audience for the speaker to read from a prepared script, make this known. High-profile

speakers are likely to encounter a wide variety of contexts, and cannot be expected to guess what kind of thing you want.

- **Will they be willing and available?** The best keynote presenters are likely to be in considerable demand. They could be in a different part of the world at the time of your planned conference. Indeed it can sometimes be necessary to plan the whole event around the availability of a key player.
- **Can you afford them?** A really good keynoter may expect a substantial fee as well as the reimbursement of travel and accommodation expenses, or you may be able to negotiate an 'expenses only' appearance. If the person concerned does ask for a fee, and is worth it, it is useful to establish exactly how much the expenditure is likely to be, so that the conference budget can be planned around such an element. Also discuss how presenters need to claim fees and expenses at this time. Many organizations need receipts against which to pay, so ensure your presenters know in advance that they need to keep these.
- **Confirm your agreement regarding fees and expenses in writing.** This will prove a useful record, especially if presenters are booked well in advance. Well-filed paperwork can eliminate difficulties arising over conflicting recollections of unrecorded telephone or face to face conversations.
- **Have you got good contact channels with keynoters?** Busy people are likely to be away from a given address, or a particular e-mail address, for periods of time, and it can be really important to make sure that you don't lose touch with your keynoters along the planning route towards the event itself.
- **Establish contact.** Speak directly to your potential keynoters to discuss your, and their, exact requirements. Provide details regarding length, potential audience (size as well as background) and the type of delivery preferred. Do you want them to provide information? Do you want them to interact with participants? How much time do you want to allow them to answer questions or engage in debate with participants?
- **Are they on all the mailing lists?** It has been known for all of the joining instructions to go to everyone else – but not to the opening keynoter! It has been known for the fact that the venue has been changed because the conference grew and grew, to reach everyone but the opening keynoter!
- **Have you heard from them that they are 'still on'?** Make sure that in the correspondence leading up to the event, you don't simply send out information to your keynoters, assuming that it's all being received and actioned. Consider issuing a formal contract to avoid being let down because something better comes along.
- **Provide a really detailed and helpful briefing for all presenters.** They are more likely to make a really positive contribution to the event if they understand what you want. Make sure someone is delegated to brief the main speakers in advance so they make a presentation that is in tune with the values and the ethos of the event. For best effect, don't rely on a single communication, but if possible, talk to them on a couple of occasions so they

have a very clear view of the nature, scope and purpose of the event. Consider sending out information about your organization, and past events, as background reading for them.

- **Brief your speakers well on the day itself.** If they are only attending for part of the day, make sure they are put in the picture about what has been said already and what will be covered later in the day.
- **A good opening.** With an opening keynote in particular, it's worth being particularly careful with the timetabling. Some minutes will be needed to open the event, welcome delegates, give housekeeping announcements, and thank the host. This opening session may well get off to a delayed start, if travel chaos has resulted in only half the expected number of delegates having arrived by kick-off time. So when the keynote itself has got under way, you need to be confident that it can finish in time for the next part of the programme to run on schedule.
- **Be particularly clear about timings.** Events can be wrecked by uncontrolled speakers who shamelessly overrun their time slots. Tell speakers their time constraints and use whatever mechanisms are appropriate to the event to enforce this rigorously. At an informal event you can use a kitchen timer set to ring when a section of the programme is complete. At more formal events you will need to have a draconian chair with charm and tact who can bring a session to its planned conclusion without cutting a speaker off half-way through a key point.
- **Aim for balance in your main speakers.** For example, you might want to balance gender and experience. Some delegates are put off from attending conferences at which the only speakers are 'white men in grey suits'. Similarly, you might want to refresh the programme by including someone from an entirely different context to the main body of your speakers: for example a student representative at a conference primarily made up of academics, or someone from a charitable body at a conference that is primarily industry/commerce focused.
- **Don't aim to include too many inputs from experts.** It can be very frustrating to attend an event at which a number of really interesting inputs are made but at which you have no opportunities to digest, discuss or debate the content.
- **Have you remembered to thank them for agreeing to contribute?** A little courtesy goes a long way, for example along the lines, 'We're really looking forward to hearing you talk about "x" on Thursday the 11th.'
- **Are they up to date with the progress of the conference planning?** Fine detail of timings, room allocations, refreshment breaks and so on often continue to develop long after the main skeleton of the conference has been designed. In addition, the actual number of delegates in a keynote session may be twice as many (or half as many) as was envisaged when the keynoters were first invited to participate. It is vital to make sure they are kept informed

of the sort of plenary room or theatre they are going to be working in, and the approximate number of faces they may expect to see there.

- **Are you going to be certain that they will be there when their slot comes up?** This is particularly important with opening keynotes. If there's travel disruption, for example, you still need to be assured that your keynoter will be there well before kick-off. One way of making sure they are there good and early is to make arrangements to take them out for a good meal on the night before the conference. This can be particularly useful if there are two or three key players at the event, and the informal discussions over dinner can make a substantial difference to the overall coherence of their respective contributions to the event.

- **Have you checked out exactly what they will need on the day?** For example, will they be using PowerPoint or an overhead projector? Are they likely to need a microphone? Do they wish to have handout materials already in delegates' hands? Do they want a printed summary to be given out after their session? Do they expect to use a lectern? And if so, is there one available? Some hotel venues are unlikely to have a lectern.

- **Try to get them to forward to you any handout materials they would like their audience to have.** This helps you get it in time to have it already in delegates' packs, as well as making it possible to upload the materials to your event Web site. Having copies in advance also gives you the opportunity to have some large-print (or Braille) copies run off for any visually impaired delegates, to allow them to follow the keynote even if they can't read the projected slides.

- **Have you built in time for them to get settled before their inputs?** Put yourself in their shoes. Few things are worse than being watched by a couple of hundred pairs of eyes as you attempt to familiarize yourself with a strange lecture room in which in a moment you will be giving your presentation, having to upload a recalcitrant PowerPoint show on to an unfamiliar computer, and to be manhandled by a technician trying to find an appropriate bit of your clothing to which to attach the mike. Make sure your keynoters have sufficient time – without delegates present – to get used to the hall, check their presentational materials and learn from the technician how best to operate any necessary technology. Otherwise the danger of mistakes increases, and hurried and harried keynoters will not feel calm and in control when they start their presentations.

- **Is there time for them to change the furniture?** Some keynoters may, for example, want to get delegates interacting in small buzz groups, and if the chairs are moveable may wish for them to be arranged in clusters rather than serried ranks. They may wish for a number of flipchart sheets to be attached strategically to the walls around the room, to allow groups of delegates to brainstorm ideas or solutions to problems.

- **Will you know them when they turn up?** Do you already know what they look like? Few things are more embarrassing for keynote speakers than to turn up at the event, stand in a long queue of delegates signing in, and for no one to know who they are. If you are entertaining keynoters before the event, it is simpler, as you can arrange to meet them at a particular place – or (better) collect them from where they are staying. If you do end up anxiously watching out for the keynoter to arrive at the start of the event, try to make sure that someone who knows them is posted as a lookout. As a fallback, advise your registration staff to inform you when they arrive, so you can make contact with them before they disappear into a heaving throng of delegates.

The wrong one

What happened?

Organizers of an international conference contacted a UK academic they knew largely from her publications, by e-mail via her publishers, to ask her to provide a keynote at an event six months hence. She agreed provisionally and was asked to provide a brief outline of her presentation, which she did, warning them at the same time that she was likely to be out of contact for a few weeks, as she was moving organizations and was unlikely to have her new e-mail account set up for a short while.

She then went very quiet for a time sufficiently long to make the conference organizer anxious. He asked his administrator to do a Web search of UK higher education institutions, to re-establish contact. The administrator set about doing this, and in due course received a draft abstract which she put up on the Web site.

Three weeks before the conference, the UK academic got in touch, rather perplexed as the abstract on the Web site was unfamiliar to her and didn't match up to her outline. With mounting horror, the organizer realized that the e-mail address of the academic was entirely different from the one provided by the person that the administrator had been corresponding with. There were two people of the same name working in similar domains, and they both thought they were giving the keynote at his conference!

What happened next?

Very carefully, the organizer contacted the author/academic by phone, checked he was speaking to the right one, owned up about what had gone wrong, and asked her to produce a new abstract for mounting on the Web site. He then had the ghastly task of disinviting the other person, who was, unsurprisingly, not at all happy, having already prepared her paper and bought her air ticket. Actually the two women knew each other, and the original one suggested that they each do a short input ('two for the price of one') but the organizer did not think this appropriate. At the conference, several delegates expressed dissatisfaction with the fact that the keynote speaker had not delivered according to her previously advertised abstract. No attempt was made to explain the situation publicly to delegates.

The learning points

What had gone wrong was that the organizers had not nailed down the contact details of the speaker right from the outset, hadn't kept contact throughout the lead-up to the process, and had not checked that the outline and abstract matched. The organizer and administrator had been working separately, and had not discussed the slightly odd tone of some of the e-mails from the second speaker, who had expressed some confusion when first contacted by the administrator by e-mail. This had been put down to language difficulties on both sides. The situation could have been retrieved by letting them both have a crack of the whip. Also, had delegates been told about the muddle, they would probably have found the situation understandable and humorous, but the opportunity was missed. A slight coolness fell between the two identically named academics.

Opening keynote where?

What happened?

The speaker had been booked to give the opening keynote at a one-day national conference in the West Midlands of the UK, organized by an educational project. The project team was based at a far corner of Britain, and had booked to stay the night before the event at a budget chain hotel in Birmingham, and fine-tune the day then, so the keynote speaker agreed to meet them there. On arrival late that night, he asked the taxi driver to take him to the named hotel in the city, but found when he got there that no booking had been made in his name and that it was already fully booked. Not knowing where to go next, he booked himself into another, more expensive hotel over the road and started to worry about where to go for the event the next day. He knew the event would be taking place at the large university in the city, but had no idea at which of the many conference venues he was due to speak.

He started ringing contacts from around 8 am (the keynote was to be 10 am). The personnel concerned with the project were all, not surprisingly, away from their various bases, as they had travelled up for the meeting, and no one back at base could advise him. He rang the university conference office, but none of the events they had booked matched the specification of the one he was seeking, and they were in many different places all around the site. He was advised to come to the conference office where he had a personal contact, and while he travelled over in the taxi the office staff rang around for him until they located the correct venue.

It transpired that the project team thought the professional body people had sent the speaker the joining instructions, and vice-versa, and no one actually had done so. No one had worked out that it might be a good idea to give him a ring on his mobile, to check that he was indeed going to turn up at the appointed place at the appointed time. They knew he'd been expecting to arrive late the previous evening, and had not worried about it, not even when he did not join them at breakfast in what turned out to be another hotel within the same chain on the very outskirts of the city!

What went wrong?

- Breakdown of communication, both between the various people organizing the event, and between them and the keynote speaker.
- Using only e-mail as a communications medium, with no other easy mechanisms to maintain contact when all the people concerned were away from their computers.
- Over-reliance on one last-minute meeting to fine-tune the programme.

The learning points

- Make sure that you know your speakers know exactly where the event is to be held. Indeed check out with them by e-mail or phone that they have received all relevant joining instructions.
- Keep to hand contact details of key people, such as mobile phone numbers, and don't hesitate to ring them up to check that everything is on track.
- Make sure joining instructions for speakers contain mobile numbers for key people on the organizing team and the venue coordinator.

Plenary sessions

We have already looked at keynotes, which are of course plenary sessions. However, many conferences and shorter events have plenary sessions that are not specifically keynotes. Such sessions – for example to introduce and close the conference or for panel discussions – are common to almost all conferences. However if not properly managed, they can prove worthless. Plenary sessions can fulfil a number of different purposes during a conference or event. The following suggestions may help you to think through how best you can manage the various kinds of plenary sessions you may build into your event.

Plenary introduction and welcome elements

It is always necessary to include some kind of introduction and welcome at the start of a conference or shorter event. This provides an opportunity to:

- set the objectives of the event in context;
- launch the start of the proceedings;
- set the tone for the conference.

This is, however, not the same as giving a keynote. Although it may be a relatively important address to the whole conference, the person launching the conference does not have to be an authority in the topic of the conference, but should have a tangible connection to the theme, or the venue, or the organization.

- **Select an individual who will be able to do all the above effectively.** If possible, this person should also be able to lend credibility to the proceedings as a result of his or her status in the organization, association or field. Aim high – most individuals, irrespective of their status, will be flattered to have been approached to kick off a conference. How about the university vice chancellor, or the chief executive, or the chair of the board, or for other events the director of a professional organization, a captain of industry or a relevant government minister?
- **Be clear from the start what you want him or her to do and how long the slot will be.** Particularly impress on the speaker the importance of keeping to time at the start of the day. You do not want your carefully constructed timetable to be out of kilter before the conference is under way, as that could lead to undesirable ramifications for the rest of the day.
- **Provide information for the introduction in the form the speaker prefers.** This may range from headings to a full text to be read out. Consider including:
  - a welcome to delegates (perhaps touching on their provenance if appropriate);

- the aim and scope of the conference;
- the structure of the day(s);
- essential information (fire exits, toilets);
- brief biographies of the next keynote the speaker could be introducing;
- housekeeping information.

However, if the opening speaker is prestigious you may be well advised not to expect him or her to do the safety or housekeeping information, so make sure someone else does this, preferably after the opening welcome address.

- **Consider letting the conference chair do the opening stages.** If appropriate, you may want the individual introducing the event to be introduced in turn by a conference chair – probably a member of the planning team. If so, this individual could perhaps also convey the housekeeping and essential information to delegates.

Panel discussion elements

Later in the conference, a plenary session comprising a panel made up of keynotes, workshop facilitators or other worthies, and the opportunity for participants to contribute from the floor, can provide a valuable opportunity for an *ad hoc* debate.

- **If you want your contributors to participate in such a session, ensure you ask them with the original invitation.** Many people will not thank you if they are thrown into such a situation without prior warning.
- **Ensure that the session is effectively chaired.** The chair has an important role in making sure that all those who wish have a chance to contribute, that points or answers are of a reasonable length and that the session runs to time.

Plenary feedback elements

A plenary session can be used very effectively for feedback (for instance, from a discussion session), as it gives all participants a chance to learn from debates that have taken place in other groups, and to interact.

- **Ensure the session is effectively chaired.** This will prevent any overrun in the feedback presentations or the session as a whole, and allow points made from the floor to be managed appropriately.
- **Brief reporters by giving clear guidelines as to what is expected of them.** This should cover time available and any limitations on the points to cover.

Plenary closure elements

In most contexts some sort of closing plenary should be included at the end of the conference, as it provides an effective way of bringing the proceedings to a formal conclusion, and of passing on essential information to participants. It is also a way of building in opportunities to thank all those who have been involved in the organization of the event. However it is necessary to ensure that the closing plenary is sufficiently interesting to encourage participants to attend. No one will be keen to attend a session that is just a roll of thanks to an enormous number of people. So how can you make this a worthwhile session?

- **Consider other inputs that could be included at this stage.** Could the session also effectively be used for:
  - a final keynote?
  - a 'wrap-up' summary of impressions/findings from the conference by an individual skilled in doing this (this is a difficult task to do well, so choose carefully)?
  - a summary of the results of the discussion sessions?
  - a chaired discussion between a panel of keynotes and the delegates?
- **Provide information to the chair to be included in the closure.** This could include:
  - details of the conference Web site, if you are creating or maintaining one;
  - dates of the next event, if it is part of a series of linked events or conferences;
  - thanks. If this is too lengthy, provide this information in the conference handbook – and refer only to the categories of those involved such as the keynotes, facilitators, technicians, conference planning team, catering staff and so on. And don't forget to include the participants – many will be pleased to have some recognition for the effort they have made to attend the conference.

Workshops and presentations

We have already looked at matters relating to keynote presentations. The main part of most events, however, consists of other presentations and workshops. Many conferences offer parallel sessions where delegates can make choices between alternative presentations or workshops. Workshops are usually an invaluable element within conferences. They provide an opportunity for participants to do what they are there for – to participate – and for conferences to do what they are organized for: to enable participants to confer. Sadly, though, many workshops belie the term, and presenters constantly hijack these sessions to provide an extended paper, to the dismay of those attending. So how can you ensure that workshops at your conference will be a truly useful experience for those attending – and facilitating? The following suggestions should help you to get the balance right. There are also sample guidance briefing notes for presenters and workshop facilitators later in this book.

- **Brief all of your presenters and facilitators well in advance.** You can do this in writing or in person, so they know what they can expect from the conference and their audience. For example, let them know how many people they are likely to have in their sessions, what is the likely background of the audience (novices, highly experienced, mixed, unknown), what the layout of the room is likely to be, and the extent to which this is flexible.
- **Think early about streaming.** If you are planning to run a series of parallel workshop sessions, try to timetable into streams to allow individuals to attend a number of workshops of interest. It is frustrating to be at a conference where you are hugely interested in five workshops running concurrently – and have no interest whatever in any of the others running before or after!
- **When you can, bring in known quantities.** If running an international, national or regional event, find your facilitators among those who are known in the field. Who is publishing in an area related to the theme of your conference? Who is providing conference sessions? Who is recommended by your team members or other peers? Select not only on the basis of their knowledge of the topic or theme but, and perhaps more importantly, their ability to facilitate an interactive workshop. If running an in-house event, find your external facilitators this way too, but also include – where possible – internal presenters to provide an opportunity for the talents and activities of staff to be showcased and disseminated. Find internals through recommendations, or perhaps by an in-house call for participation.
- **Make clear to workshop presenters what you want them to do.** In particular let them know how you want them to balance presentation and discussion. If you want the sessions to be interactive, make it clear that it is unacceptable for them to use up all the available time presenting. If they are paper presentation sessions, establish whether questions and interruptions are acceptable during the presentation.
- **Make it clear what sorts of session are which.** For example, emphasize that the 'work' in workshops refers to participation by delegates. One of the most common complaints in conferences is that some of the workshops were just papers with (and sometimes without) an opportunity for questions tacked on at the end. Speak to your facilitators before the session to ensure that they have built in true interactive opportunities.
- **Provide an adequate timescale for workshops.** The length of time allocated will depend on the intended outcomes of the session and the activity to be achieved. However 60–90 minutes is usually a suitable timescale for workshop elements. If you choose a longer duration, timetable a break and ensure plenty of refreshments are to hand.

- **Discuss your requirements for the sessions with the facilitators.** Be clear about what you want in terms of both content and delivery. Reinforce the 'work' in workshops, and ask what interactive opportunities they intend to provide. Use the right terminology to get the message home: facilitator not presenter, participant not attendee, workshop not presentation.
- **Ask your presenters to provide you with suitable detail about their proposed sessions.** You will need such detail if you are organizing a committee or planning group to select which workshops and presentations will be accepted into the conference programme, and which will be turned down. The suggestions for workshop facilitators towards the end of this book may help you decide upon exactly what you will need to know from would-be facilitators to help you select the best offerings. Such detail should ideally lend itself to inclusion in due course in the conference handbook, if you are intending to provide one.
- **Discuss optimum numbers for workshops in advance with facilitators.** This helps you to enable interactivity at workshops, and to suit these elements to the time and space available. It is useful to ask them for minimum and maximum numbers. If there turns out to be less demand for a workshop than the minimum number specified by the facilitator, it is usually best to cancel it, rather than have a few disappointed delegates trying to work out which session to go into late – or whether to just miss the rest of the conference slot concerned. If there is more demand than the suggested maximum number, it can be better to find out whether the facilitator is willing and able to repeat the session during the conference, rather than end up with an uncomfortably full workshop room, with inadequate opportunity for real interaction. Your facilitator, if expecting to run an interactive session with a maximum of 12, will not thank you for being required to attempt the same session with 60, with the majority sitting on tables, the floor or each other. Your participants will not find it a useful session either. Once agreed, limit numbers to these agreed quotas by using signing-up sheets and briefing the chair – if necessary – to eject those not on it.
- **Plan ahead for breakout rooms to maximize interactivity.** Organize the main workshop room in a horseshoe or similar shape, to provide an opportunity for the facilitator to start and lead proceedings, and for those present to participate easily in planned workshop activities and discussion. Where necessary arrange that smaller breakout groups can use adjacent rooms, where it is not possible for the main workshop group to subdivide satisfactorily in the main room.
- **Manage expectations about presentation equipment.** If you cannot supply data projectors for all the parallel sessions, it is best to be upfront about this, rather than let presenters prepare elaborate materials in advance and then get fed up because you cannot provide them with the equipment they need to use.

- **Let them know what you can and cannot do about handouts.** The bane of the desk staff's life at a conference is the presenter seeking last-minute copying. If this is unlikely to be easy, tell presenters in advance that they will need to bring their own handouts (give a rough guide how many), tell them there will be facilities for them to make copies themselves at the conference on a pay-per-page basis, or suggest that they provide handouts electronically after the event. If paper handouts are an expectation at a conference and you have a low proportion of international presenters, you may wish to make exceptions in their cases to save their luggage allowances.
- **If possible, provide chairs for the workshop sessions.** Their role is likely to include: introducing speakers, monitoring that presenters are abiding by the ground rules, keeping time, handling questions according to the presenters' wishes and thanking them at the end. You also need chairs to sort out any problems that arise, such as technical problems with equipment, insufficient seating, and individuals turning up beyond the limit. Select a chair who will be able to fulfil all these roles and will be sufficiently assertive to ensure the session finishes on time. Chairs for workshops (and indeed for other sessions) should be briefed beforehand – see the guidelines towards the end of this book for thoughts about briefing notes. Be clear about what you want them to do, or not do. Impress on them the importance of concluding the session on time even if it is unfinished.

Discussion sessions

These sessions provide an invaluable opportunity for participants to interact with the key issues of the conference in a meaningful and practical way. Discussion sessions can be used at major conferences to provide depth to the content, and also in internal events to agree on an institutional stance on a new issue, or to identify areas requiring development and support. If properly run, these sessions can go very well, with the resulting discussion being much greater than the sum of the parts. But they can go horribly wrong if they are not properly managed. So how can you make discussion session useful?

- **Timetable discussion sessions at appropriate points in the overall conference.** Often after the first keynote is a good time, as participants should – hopefully – now have a shared platform of knowledge and be inspired to take up a position on the issues.
- **Ensure the right length for the session.** If it is too short, participants may have barely begun to tackle the issues. If it is too long, participants may feel they are covering the ground too slowly and that their time at the conference is being wasted. It's a fine line!

- **Think through optimum numbers.** These sessions only work if there are sufficient numbers present to allow a cross-section of opinion. Conversely too many people at a discussion session will formalize proceedings, and many may feel that they have not had the opportunity to have their way.
- **Be clear about the objectives of the session.** Provide an activity sheet in everyone's pack indicating what you want them to discuss, and in what form the intended outputs from the discussion should be reported.
- **Provide the necessary equipment.** This could include flip-chart paper and stand, sticky notes, pens, and perhaps also an overhead projector (remember to supply blank transparencies too) or a video recorder.
- **Manage the proceedings by organizing a chair and a reporter.** It is preferable to appoint these people beforehand. You will save valuable debating time during the sessions if participants don't first have to agree on who is to carry out these roles (a particularly difficult task if participants don't know each other). You can also be assured that you have individuals in place who you know are able to do the job, who are forewarned of their involvement, and who have agreed to take on the task. The chair's job is to ensure that the discussion remains on track, to ensure that anyone who wants to speak has an opportunity to do so, and to work towards the objectives of the session being met. The reporter's job is to summarize the discussions and to present the results in written or oral (or both) form as required.
- **Trigger the discussion by using some stimulus such as a short video.** Using some sort of a trigger like this will help break the ice among participants (who may not already know each other), encapsulate the issues you wish discussed, and stimulate individuals to put forward their views.
- **Organize the room to maximize discussion.** A tiered lecture room will not allow the interaction you seek. Organize the room with seating in a horseshoe or circular shape to encourage all present to feel they are contributing on an equal basis.
- **Provide an opportunity to feed back the results of the discussion.** The traditional way for this feedback to be presented is a in a plenary session by reporters. However the results can be deadly if they are not properly managed: for example, if a series of frustrated speakers present the findings at length – often giving their own opinions – rather than the groups' views. Alternative methods can include:
  - the provision of ideas on a flip-chart or series of sticky notes for later examination by participants on an individual basis (advertise well where these are to be displayed);
  - the reporting of only a limited number of issues (perhaps only one) in plenary;
  - the inclusion of results in post-conference literature, or perhaps a conference Web site with a forum facility to encourage and enable continuity of discussion among participants.

Networking sessions

Such elements can be most useful at conferences of professional associations, where members only have the opportunity to meet together from time to time, and where they may wish to follow up themes of mutual interest arising from the conference or from other developments relating to their association. Such sessions provide an opportunity for participants to discuss areas of common concern, and structures that can lead to collaborative ventures or future partnerships. Many people attending conferences find networking elements really valuable, sometimes more so than the formal sessions which you have laboriously constructed for their benefit. The following suggestions may help you make the most of networking opportunities at your conference, rather than have the conference interrupted by delegates skipping sessions to network.

- **Consider timetabling these sessions.** This will provide an opportunity for them to take place during the event, rather than at the side of the event, and also help ensure that all those with a common interest can be free at the same time to maximize the benefit of the discussion.
- **Don't squeeze them.** For example, don't plan a networking element of a conference between the closing plenary on day 2 and the conference dinner. Delegates may be tired, and eager to change for dinner, and just have a break to wind down ready for the social side of the day. A networking opportunity at such a time may be the last thing they are looking for.
- **Advertise the sessions in advance publicity.** Awareness of this opportunity may well have a beneficial effect on registration. Where possible, include some prompts or questions to start delegates thinking ahead to the sorts of issues where networking may be most valuable or timely.
- **Consider having a 'Networking' notice board.** For example, encourage delegates to post messages on this board about matters they believe like-minded delegates may like to debate and address at a networking session. This can be a way of informally establishing a suitable agenda for such sessions.
- **If appropriate, manage networking sessions by arranging a structure to the sessions, together with a chair and a reporter.** Do this in much the same way as that suggested for the discussion sessions detailed above.
- **Consider providing refreshments.** Networking can often be done even better armed with tea or coffee and biscuits. Planning a networking opportunity into an area normally used for refreshments can be a way of attracting people to participate more readily.
- **Don't make networking compulsory.** Networking should be a relatively spontaneous process, and any element of compulsion can damage this. Also if delegates are forced into a networking process, and it turns out not to work well, they can become resentful of the time they feel they have wasted

on the process, and indicate that they would have preferred conventional conference sessions instead.

- **Remember those who may not be part of the network.** For example, if there is an element of 'members only' at some kinds of networking sessions, any delegates who don't happen to be members can feel alienated and isolated. Try always to have something interesting for those who may prefer not to be involved in networking elements – for example a visit to a poster display or commercial exhibition, or an informal session for 'fringe' delegates.

Poster exhibitions

It is increasingly common for relatively large or popular conferences to include poster exhibitions or displays. For example, contributors to a conference may not wish to present a formal paper, or to run a workshop, or to lead a discussion, but may prefer to provide an 'exhibit'. Alternatively, where there are too many people wanting to contribute papers and workshops at a conference, those whose offerings are not accepted for the main programme can be given the option of contributing to a poster display. Exhibitions can form an excellent dimension to a conference by providing ancillary information, live exhibits, and providing an opportunity for staff at an in-house event to showcase good practice. The following checklist of questions, along with accompanying suggestions, may help you to get the most out of such a display, and minimize the risks. You may also find it useful to look at the tips on organizing commercial exhibitions which follow on from the present set.

- **Decide whether you really will have room for a poster display.** If providing a poster is likely to become a popular delegate choice, the exhibition space requirements could get out of hand. If you are paying for space as used at a commercially-run conference venue, the costs of mounting a poster display could be very significant, and needs to be thought through carefully in terms of the overall budget for the event.
- **How will a poster display fit in with other exhibitions?** For example, if the conference is also going to include a 'trade' exhibition (with stands being provided – and paid for – by publishers, resource designers, and others with something to sell to delegates), will it be necessary to separate the commercial display from the conference-related topic display? The borderline between commercial and subject-based displays is sometimes unclear; even a topic-based poster is likely to be 'selling' some research or development ideas to delegates.
- **Site an exhibition where it will be seen.** Perhaps the exhibition can share the same accommodation as the refreshments, to allow individuals to view it over coffee and lunch breaks. Your exhibitors will be very unhappy (and

unlikely to input at future events) if they are hived away into some peaceful part of the venue where delegates rarely venture.

- **Make the exhibition space available early.** Ensure that the display area is available for contributors to set up displays in advance of the conference. Registration is often a good time for participants to view displays – not to see them being assembled.

- **Ensure you have plenty of stationery supplies on the day.** Velcro, sticky fixers, drawing pins, and many more bits and pieces will be requested by exhibitors setting up their displays. Work out what quantities of such things you think will be needed – and then triple them!

- **Decide the specification you will adopt for posters.** It is important that they all conform to the same overall specification, particularly overall area to be used. The smallest realistic area is the size of a single flip-chart sheet (A1), and a reasonable maximum (especially if the exhibition is going to be fairly full) is probably around four such sheets.

- **Will you need to be more specific about the style and format for posters?** For example, depending on the nature of your display space, it's worth thinking about whether the posters should be readable from a metre or two away, perhaps with tables in front of them upon which printed materials, handouts, and other material can be mounted. This could lead you to make decisions about specifying a minimum print size for the posters, to ensure that they can be viewed satisfactorily by several people at a time, from a reasonable distance.

- **Are you likely to have contributors who wish for a multimedia poster?** For example, at exhibitions of resource materials, exhibits tend more often than not to be multimedia, with hands-on computer options for passing delegates, and so on. For a poster display option at a conference, the added complications of having multimedia display possibilities are considerable. There are issues about the supply of power to the technology, about cabling and safety, about noise and sound levels, and not least about security, for example at times when the exhibition is unstaffed.

- **Think about display stands.** Can you provide these? If so, can you provide enough of them? Will you provide them free of charge, or will you rent them? Will you invite presenters to bring their own display stands with them? And if so, how will you make it fair if some bring bigger and better stands than others? Who will be responsible if their property gets lost, damaged or stolen?

- **Will walls do?** Sometimes a conference venue has suitable rooms with blank walls lending themselves to fix posters temporarily with Blu-tack or similar adhesives. But beware – if the walls get marked or damaged, the bill for repair or redecoration could come back to you.

- **For how long will the exhibition be available to delegates?** It is normally best for it to be timetabled into the overall conference, so that there is a definite time and place for delegates to visit the exhibition. For obvious reasons, it's best that any poster exhibition is timetabled around the middle of the conference rather than near the beginning or end, since exhibitors are likely to arrive and leave at different times.

- **Will the posters be 'staffed' at set times, or will it be a stand-alone exhibition?** It usually works best when there is the opportunity for delegates to circulate around a poster exhibition and talk to those whose exhibits interest them. However, the exhibitors themselves will be joining in conference sessions, and will certainly not wish to be on duty beside their exhibits for long periods of time. It is worth thinking how best to get a reasonable number of people at the exhibition at planned times.

- **Consider timetabling the exhibition into the conference.** This will provide an opportunity for individuals to take time to view the displays of interest to them. It will also provide a limited time during which displayers can stand beside their displays to answer questions and discuss their posters with delegates. This type of activity is particularly valuable to staff new to presenting their work at conference, and who appreciate this opportunity as valuable experience before going on to present papers and other sessions in future years.

- **When else may delegates find the time to visit the posters?** Where a poster exhibition is effectively serving as an 'overflow' to capture the surplus contributions that were originally offered as papers or presentations, the programme is already likely to be congested with parallel sessions, and most of the available time will be timetabled. But unless some dedicated time is allocated to visiting the exhibition, it could end up a lonely place. It does not really work to choose such dedicated time as the gap between the end of the last session on the middle day and the conference dinner, as delegates will normally prefer to dress up for the dinner, or have a pre-dinner drink somewhere. However, if that pre-dinner drink could happen to be provided in the exhibition area; see below.

- **Consider having an event in the exhibition area.** For example, a glass of wine for all comers, backed by a sponsor, can be a means of getting a substantial number of delegates into the poster exhibition area at a time when the exhibitors themselves are likely to be free to be present too.

- **How will the posters get to the venue?** Will delegates wish to send them in advance? If so, who will unpack, sort and store them, and arrange for them to be at the venue at the right time and in the right place?

- **Who will put the posters up?** Will you leave this to the delegates who have provided them? If so, how will you deal with the early birds choosing the most favourable positions, and so on? Will delegates need (or expect) some help in putting up their posters? (They are more likely to expect help if they are paying for their space.) If so, will there be an unmanageable surge in the need for such help?

- **Who will take the posters down after the event?** Will they all be taken down at about the same time, or will different delegates want to remove them when they have finished with them, or when they are about to leave the conference?

Clearly, a poster exhibition works much better if no one is putting up or taking down exhibits while the exhibition is in full use.

- **What else should be supplied alongside the posters?** It can be useful to suggest that it is up to exhibitors to provide a one-page flier to go with their poster, which can be taken by those delegates interested in it. Such fliers need to bear contact details, and if possible a useful digest or summary of the work being presented by the poster.

- **What else should you think of including in the conference handbook?** For example, it can be useful to provide a page or two containing the titles of the accepted exhibits, the contact details of the exhibitors, and possibly a very short abstract of each exhibit. The problem is that this could be one of the most 'fuzzy' areas of the conference, in that it might be quite late before all the details needed for such pages became available. Moreover there could well be offers of posters that do not turn into exhibits, and indeed delegates who have not 'booked' to set up a poster who decide that they wish to do so during the conference itself, possibly encouraged by the reaction to their presentations or workshops.

Commercial exhibitions

Such exhibitions can range enormously in size, scope and purpose. At some conferences, the exhibition is an event in its own right, often with free tickets to the exhibition being issued to (for example) members of the professional association putting on the conference. Free tickets to the exhibition may also be circulated by exhibitors themselves to tempt people to the show. In such cases, the fees for attending the conference sessions and social events are handled quite separately, with careful ticketing and admission procedures being necessary. The suggestions below, however, apply to the more usual scenario, where a relatively small-scale commercial exhibition is set up alongside a conference, and delegates are free to visit it. There is of course some overlap between the steps needed to make commercial exhibitions work, and those relating to poster displays, but we revisit key points from our previous list here, for those who are only considering commercial exhibitions.

- **Turf wars create a bad impression.** Make sure you have told each exhibitor clearly what space and facilities will be available. Establish early what power supply or Internet connection each might require. If you have not allowed adequate space for each exhibitor – or made clear how much space will be available – early arrivals will encroach on neighbours' spaces, who in turn will bring the problem to the conference team. If your exhibitors have free-standing display systems, find out the exact dimensions and notify them early if there will be difficulties accommodating them. Halfway through set-up is not the time for you or the exhibitor to discover that the ceiling is too low or the display booth too narrow.

- **Exhibitionists want to be seen.** Your exhibitors are paying for exposure, to be seen, to make a visual impact on your delegates, so tucking them away in a far corner of a third floor landing is not going to please them. The space may be perfectly proportioned, self-contained and convenient (for you), but unless your delegates are forced through the space in search of refreshments or on the way to their next session they may go through the whole event blissfully unaware of the exhibition.

- **Make the most of social spaces.** If possible locate your exhibition in one of the social spaces of your event, a lounge where coffee is served for example, so that delegates feel comfortable, not harassed, and free to approach the stands. If your venue insists your exhibition is located in a side room, give your delegates additional reasons for visiting, like constant self-serve refreshments, sign-up sheets for sessions or a general information point.

- **Delegates don't want the hard sell.** While most delegates recognize that commercial exhibitors help to finance the event and might also introduce them to potentially useful goods and services, they will not appreciate being pounced on by over-enthusiastic sales people. The exhibitors will often have gone on training courses about working an exhibition, and might try to adopt strategies for attracting attention that will be perceived at best as intrusive and at worst wholly inappropriate to a non-commercial conference, for example an academic event.

- **Provide exhibitors with appropriate guidance notes in advance.** Explain to them what kind of conference or event it is intended to be, what to expect, and how best to 'work' the exhibition, for example in the context of an academic or scholarly event. Make clear your expectations of them, and manage their expectations of your event.

- **A delegate list is not a marketing list for exhibitors.** Whatever your exhibitors have paid for, they have not bought the rights to your delegates' personal information. You should make sure that your delegate list only includes details of those individuals who have explicitly given you permission to publish their information. Beware of assuming that just because every event you have ever attended has shared your contact details with all the delegates, it is all right for you to do the same. The data protection regulations are increasingly stringent, and you should only be distributing personal information if individuals have given explicit informed consent. Leave your exhibitors to collect 'contacts' who are genuinely interested in their products and services.

- **Variety is the spice of life.** It may seem incongruous to locate commercial and conference content exhibitors together, but it may actually make for a more dynamic exhibition. It is often very difficult to categorize organizations clearly, and a number of public sector agencies, subject associations, professional bodies and charities will happily share an exhibition hall with educational software developers, publishers, consultants and the like.

- **Think carefully where to site different kinds of exhibition.** Take care to cluster your stands sensitively, taking account of whether a stand will attract significant numbers of browsers (especially book stands) or whether individuals may prefer a quieter location with opportunity for more one-to-one discussion. Remember that publishers scout for new authors at academic conferences, so you may do everyone a favour locating academic posters where the publishers can see them without straying far from their own stand.
- **Think about the differences.** If, for example, you are organizing a poster display and at the same time a commercial exhibition, you are likely to be charging the commercial exhibitors considerably more than the delegates who choose to set up a display – indeed you may not be charging at all for this. However the borderlines between a small commercial display and an ambitious delegate display are quite blurred, and you need to ensure that neither category feels inappropriately treated, either financially or in terms of space, location and visibility.
- **There's always one!** The 'one' may be the novice exhibitor who loses all the takings by leaving the stand unattended, or the determined salesperson who leaves no member of your team unharassed until gaining possession of your delegate list. Do whatever you can to anticipate problems from your exhibitors, and be ready to handle challenges from them just as thoroughly as from your delegates.

Determined to be seen

What happened?

The lift was too small to take all the display materials in one trip, and three flights of stairs were not a realistic alternative. There was no porter available to help, and the venue staff seemed uncertain about the event taking place. After two trips in the lift it stopped working for no apparent reason, and an hour passed before a maintenance engineer could arrive to repair it.

Hot and flustered, the exhibitor finally got all the materials to the third floor. The area designated for the exhibition was at the narrow end of a triangular balcony/gallery. Exhibition booths had been erected along the two longest sides of the triangle, with an additional island of back-to-back booths in the middle. The booths were of conventional structure, and came supplied with two spotlights already plugged in and switched on. All seemed fine, if a little cramped, until the exhibitor tried erecting a free-standing display system. The system popped up with its usual flourish and came to an abrupt stop, not quite fully extended, one side wedged

---

against the side of the booth, the back pressed against the now scorching hot spotlights. The exhibitor, daunted but not deterred, managed to manipulate the display diagonally across the front of the booth. It overshot the allocated space but by this time the exhibitor didn't care.

Once settled the exhibitor sat in wait for hordes of visitors... and waited... and waited. A few hardy individuals ventured towards the displays, but backed away hastily when confronted with what looked like an ambush from a spaghetti western: brochure-toting desperados leering at the potential visitors from the narrow gorge of banners, posters and electronic gizmos.

After a day and a half and only a trickle of visitors, all trying to look at the displays without actually making eye contact with the exhibitors, the most determined exhibitor started asking the conference organizer for a delegate list. When refused, he asked one of the clerical team. Again refused, he asked a steward who, trying to be helpful, apologized for the omission and gave him a complete list of all the delegates with their contact details.

What did we learn?

Make sure the exhibition space is adequate, not just in size, but in shape, ambiance, access, everything. If you provide power or light, do not leave the electricals switched on and 'live'. Hot spotlights are a hazard, so leave exhibitors to switch them on when they are ready.

Ensure adequate porterage so that exhibitors can be assisted with their equipment if necessary. Remember many organizations, commercial and not-for-profit, will send only one person to an exhibition, and whether male or female, they often struggle with heavy boxes, display equipment and so on.

Exhibitors will want their money's worth, one way or another. If plenty of visitors go to the exhibition, the representatives will collect legitimate information from people really interested in their products and services, and will not have to resort to acquiring 'contacts' by dubious means.

Make sure all your staff and venue staff are fully briefed. Venue staff need to know what's going on if they are to be helpful. Make friends with the venue reception staff and they will generally be more helpful to your delegates and exhibitors.

Be very clear about who has what information, and who is allowed to give it to whom. You will not endear yourself to your delegates if they receive unsolicited marketing materials from exhibitors after your event.

4 Early planning

Most of this book is about planning in one way or another. It would have been satisfying if we could have had a logical and sequential approach, with planning running from the idea of putting on a conference or event, right through to the final review of the event after it had happened.

To some extent, we have tried to provide a sequential 'walk through' the overall picture of planning, delivering and evaluating an event in this book. However, life is not so straightforward as to be sequential and one-directional. In fact many of the sub-sections throughout the rest of this book contain their own 'before, during and after' components.

We therefore suggest that you dip into the remainder of this book, cherry-picking those aspects that are particularly relevant to your own situation, and skimming over those parts which are not relevant. The elements we have included in this section on 'early planning' are:

- when your event will be held;
- choosing your venue;
- convening your team;
- leading a conference team;
- developing your project plan;
- costing the event;
- marketing;
- promoting your event;
- sponsorship.

When your event will be held

Choosing a date for your event can be critical to its success, as potential contributors and participants will be unable to attend if it is scheduled to coincide with a predictable peak in their working year, with already diaried dates, or if it conflicts with other events of interest to them. The following suggestions may help you to plan an optimum time for your particular event.

- **If organizing an internal event, check your own organization's calendar first.** This will ensure that the conference is held at a time when the majority of the participants you wish to attract will be available.
- **Also check the availability of key facilities and resources.** There's nothing worse than finding out too late that your best conference rooms – and the catering provision – have already been reserved for another conference.
- **Check dates you have selected with a handful of potential participants.** Sometimes an organizational calendar will not show activities that will keep your client group away (for example in educational institutions, post-examination marking periods, or scheduled staff development time which has been hived off by departments or sections for their own away-day and team building purposes).
- **If organizing a local, national or international event, check what else may be going on which could keep delegates away.** Do your dates conflict with holidays (for example, local holidays in Scotland, Spring and August bank holidays in England and Wales, school holiday periods)? Could there be a significant conflict with the dates of religious events or traditions (such as Easter, Thanksgiving, Ramadan)? Are there other important events looming up which could affect delegates' willingness to be at a conference at your chosen time (for example, major sporting happenings such as a World Cup final, or significant national events like a Royal wedding)?
- **Check appropriate Web sites for possible conflicts with similar events.** For instance, professional associations, staff development providers or other networks may also be holding an event on the same or a similar date to yours. Your participants are unlikely to have the time, resources or stamina to attend back-to-back events, and yours may be the loser.
- **Continue to check out dates with some potential participants from your client group.** Otherwise it is only when your event has been organized and the publicity has gone out that some kind person will let you know of a conflict which could decimate your delegate numbers.
- **Decide on an appropriate duration and timing for residential events.** Residential events tend to be held for around three days. You will have to decide if this is a sensible duration or if it will be too costly for your participants in terms of fees, subsistence costs and time away from the office.
- **Can you make a three-day residential conference the equivalent of more than one self-contained event?** For those unable to attend the whole conference, will it work to provide opportunities for one-day enrolment? This will require you to have an attractive and coherent programme available for each of the conference days, and to disseminate this programme in good time to enable one-day delegates to make an informed choice.
- **Decide the appropriate time of the week for residential events.** Would a mid-week event be the most suitable for your particular purposes? Or would a residential weekend event be attractive to participants? If your conference location is also an attractive tourist venue, would it pay to have the

conference at the start or finish of a week, so that delegates could choose to add on a holiday weekend to the conference?

- **Try to find a date that suits the majority of your participants.** But be aware that whatever date you choose will not suit everyone – as you will be informed many times over.
- **Are there ways of satisfying those who just can't attend?** It can be worthwhile to find a way for those unable to attend in person to engage in the content of your event, perhaps through your Web site, or by provision of papers and mailings that include advance information of the date of the next event you are planning. This year's non-attender could be next year's fee-paying delegate.

Choosing your venue

You may have no choice – it could be at your place, and that's that! Even so, however, it's worth thinking through how well the venue matches your purposes. If you do have a choice of venue, before examining alternative options, consider fully what your needs are. The location of your event can affect – either beneficially or adversely – the number of participants who attend, the extent and nature of the input within the conference, and the overall feel of the event. The following suggestions may help you to work out the pros and cons of some of the options you could need to think about, and perhaps find your dream venue – or at least the next best thing.

- **Start early.** Most good venues are booked well in advance, and you may find it difficult to secure the one you desire if you leave the booking too late.
- **Analyse what size of venue you need.** How many participants do you anticipate? What types of input are you considering? How large a hall will you require for plenary events? How many breakout rooms will you need for workshop or seminar rooms – and what size will they need to be? If there is an exhibition associated with the event, can this be sited effectively? If there is an associated social programme, is there space for elements within it to be held at the venue?
- **List what facilities you will require.** What computer and other audio-visual facilities will you need? Is Internet access available in the rooms where it will be required? Can audio-visual equipment be set up easily? Is wheeled access for heavy equipment possible? Are the rooms suitable for data projection? What catering facilities do you require? Will you require participants to be served meals on site? Where will coffee and tea be served?
- **Ensure the venue is accessible to all.** A surprising number of possible venues are only partly accessible for wheelchair users. Ensure your venue is fully accessible to ensure your conference programme is entirely open to all participants. Reject venues that are not accessible, and be explicit about why

you do so. It is only by taking such action that those seeking to rent out venues will realize that they will have to invest in adapting their premises if they wish to continue to secure business.

- **Consider what environment you want.** Do you want to build in plenty of networking and informal discussion opportunities? If so, ensure your venue is suitably arranged to facilitate this, perhaps with a central area where participants can meet up, and where there is plenty of comfortable seating and self-help refreshments.
- **Consider the costs fully.** Ensure all elements have been costed in when you agree the price. This will avoid a nasty shock and arguments later.
- **If organizing an institutional event, weigh up carefully the pros and cons of an on- or off-site event.** Consider the benefits of using in-house facilities (at cost, or perhaps at no cost at all) as against external facilities (at market rates). An on-site event can have the disadvantage of being too close to home. Sessions may be held so close to participants' rooms that they are unable to resist the pull of their e-mail in-boxes or overflowing in-tray. As a result they may miss vital parts of the day – or never return. On the plus side, the familiarity of the location to you and the participants, together with your control over it, may make this the best option for you.
- **If organizing a local event, consider carefully which would be the best location for the participants you hope to attract.** Is the venue close enough to public transport facilities for individuals to reach it by train, tube or bus if they wish? If they choose to come by car, is there parking anywhere close by and at a reasonable cost? Once you decide on your venue, you will have to advise participants of the available options, to enable them to make good choices about their mode of transport. Be careful to time your start and finish to enable people to use the available transport to arrive and leave on time – or you may find your keynote is talking to a cold empty hall or no one is left for the conference close.
- **If organizing a national event, select a location that is accessible at reasonable cost to the majority of your participants.** Be aware that with cut-price airline fares, delegates living at a distance from London may find it easier to travel there than a halfway house option which actually involves more expensive and time-consuming travel options. Be realistic about the centrality of your venue. Although you may be keen to reward participants living at a distance for dogged attendance over a number of years at annual conferences by arranging an event in their locality, only do this if you can guarantee reasonable attendance from participants living centrally. Those who live centrally may not be so adventurous or enterprising on the travel front as those who live remotely and accept travelling a distance as a fact of life. It is well known round the UK that people travel to London from distant parts much more readily than from the London area to the provinces.
- **If organizing an international event, the location may be obvious as each member of the organizing committee takes a turn in shouldering the**

responsibility. However, take care that venues chosen will not be too difficult to reach, expensive to participate in, or in an international hot-spot that is likely to deter your delegates from other nations. Again, realism is necessary if costly mistakes resulting from low participation are to be avoided.

- **If there is an associated social programme, investigate what is at or near this location which you could usefully include.** Are there local landmarks or sights where visits could be made? Are there venues that could host a reception or conference dinner?
- **Use tourist boards, councils and other sources of information.** They will often be really helpful in offering you advice about venues in their locality, and suggesting facilities you may use. They may even be willing to provide some sponsorship – or at least free leaflets about the region or city to include in your delegate pack.
- **Do some research, if thinking of an unusual location.** Track down someone who has organized an event there recently, and try and talk to them, well primed with a list of questions to ask. For example ask them, 'What were the best things about the location in practice?' and 'What turned out to be the worst things?'
- **Consider using a venue-finding organization.** You could recoup the cost in terms of legwork saved.
- **Location isn't everything.** In the final analysis, don't forget that wherever your event is located, it is people who make the place work for the event. There is little point selecting the best venue facilities in a perfect geographical location, if the venue staff turn out to be intransigent and unhelpful. How you are treated by the venue staff when you are researching your choice of location can be an indicator of how they will respond to your delegates. Look for a 'can do' attitude rather than a 'jobsworth' culture (for example when they tell you, 'We don't do it like that here!' when you make a suggestion). Remember that it's your event, and you are the paying customer.

When is a venue really accessible?

What happened?

An organization that really prides itself on putting good equal opportunities policy into practice booked a venue for a conference with assurances that all areas were accessible to those with mobility problems. Before booking the venue, the conference planning team carefully checked all areas including lecture theatres, seminar rooms, eating and social areas and toilets.

On arrival at the venue the team 'walked the talk' again because they knew they had a booking from a wheelchair user. Everything seemed fine.

Their own reception desk was too high for the disabled participant to use comfortably, but the registration team were briefed for one of them to step out to the side of the desk to register the participant at a conveniently placed low side table.

There were some minor problems about getting the wheelchair through circulation areas when these were full, but the crunch really came when the participant tried to go into the room for the first seminar he had signed up for. This was in a large room that had been partitioned into two with a folding wall. His wheelchair was about an inch too wide to fit through the doorway into the second area. For a moment, confusion reigned and the organizers were really upset. However, the venue managers were summoned hastily, rapidly disassembled a section of the partition wall to let him in, and stood by to let him out again at the end of the workshop. They too were embarrassed because never previously had they had a wheelchair user in the room when it was partitioned, so they hadn't realized there was likely to be a problem.

Learning points

- It is advisable for all event organizers to check and double-check accessibility for those who have mobility restrictions.
- Common problems include venues 'forgetting' that there are likely to be small areas of mainly accessible venues that are inaccessible to some users, such as slight changes in the level of large rooms, and doorways that can probably accommodate an empty wheelchair, but not one that is occupied.
- Doorways with springs on them, toilet areas that look big enough but don't have enough space to enable a wheelchair to turn around, and heavy external doors that are barriers to people unable to push and pull sufficiently strongly are all surprisingly common.
- In addition, venues often make participant areas accessible but forget that the speaker may be a wheelchair user, so have unsuitably high lecterns and demonstration benches, or even have the speaker's position on a dais that it is impossible to mount without using steps.
- Be aware that some people have hidden disabilities like heart disease and asthma, and you may also have temporarily disabled participants, such as those who have broken a leg since they booked for the conference, and may not have thought to tell you.

Convening your team

Organizing and running a conference is essentially a team operation. The team charged with the responsibility of planning the conference is likely to include both colleagues to advise and individuals employed to assist in various ways. The team at the event is often significantly different from the team that planned the event. The right composition of the team is essential to ensure the conference is thoughtfully planned, effective decisions are made and the necessary work is done. But where can you find such valuable people? The following suggestions may help you to find your key players, and keep good team work going, particularly when the pressure is on.

- **Start recruiting your team really early.** The sooner you can decide on the members of the team, the more likely those useful people you want to include on it will be able to make arrangements to ensure their future availability.
- **Many hands make light work and too many cooks spoil the broth.** Mix your metaphors! Make sure you have the right sized team of the right people. One or two people generating ideas and shaping the scope and theme of the event will be valuable; too many bright ideas will undermine a coherent approach and lead to confusion in the execution of the event. Likewise ensure you have enough people undertaking the administration of the event, checking bookings, making sure joining instructions go out on time, and so on.
- **Encourage individuals to volunteer.** Working with individuals keen to contribute will be much more successful than working with those who have been press-ganged to help.
- **Ensure your team is of a manageable size.** You want a team that is not too small to carry the responsibility, and not too large or it will be unwieldy and unable to reach good collective decisions.
- **Remember that your event team is likely to include people outside your organization and control.** You should be in close contact with a representative of the host venue. If you are using your own organization this may be a colleague in the estates department or its equivalent; if you are using an external venue like a hotel or conference centre you should be working with a designated contact person. Take the time to build an effective working relationship with these people – you will be entirely at their mercy for many aspects of the event.
- **A camel is a horse designed by committee.** There is tremendous value in utilizing experts and enthusiasts from outside your organization to help plan an event, but be very clear about the role you envisage for these colleagues, and the expectations they have for their involvement.
- **Ensure you brief team members adequately from the start regarding their likely time commitment.** This will include time in terms of attendance at

meetings, their area of responsibility as well as any requirement to assist at the conference itself. It is essential that there is transparency here – team members do not want to sign up for an open-ended commitment.

- **Ask members to ensure they are free to attend the event.** Perhaps this is obvious to some, but unfortunately not to all! However well intentioned people may be, if they know they are not going to be there on the day they won't put in as much effort.
- **Include on the team only those prepared to attend meetings and to shoulder an area of responsibility.** This is essential for the whole process to be workable. A conference team is a busy group of people, and there is no room for passengers, or people who are full of ideas but without any intention of helping their ideas come to fruition.
- **Make it as easy as possible for team members to fulfil their roles.** For instance, planning meetings can be arranged to take place at midday with a sandwich lunch provided, or clerical assistance can be offered if needed.
- **Be careful not to overload individuals.** In particular try not to give any particular individuals so much to do at the conference that their participation and engagement with it is limited. They are likely to have joined the planning team because of their interest in the theme, so will be keen to be involved as a participant, both to learn more of an area of interest and to witness the fruition of their hard work in terms of a successful event.
- **Maximize the payoff of time spent together.** Ensure that meetings do not become limited to presentation of progress. Continue to use them to debate issues, revisit plans and get fresh ideas throughout the lead-up to the event.
- **If possible, include individuals with a range of experience in the planning process.** Working with individuals you have successfully worked with before will allow you to be confident, and also provide them with an opportunity to develop and hone their skills further. Including others new to planning will also be worthwhile – provided they are given responsibilities commensurate with their experience and present abilities and appropriate support. Today's new recruits may well be tomorrow's conference organizers.
- **Ensure you have complementary skills.** While it is invaluable to have a visionary on the team who can inspire and shape the event, a team of visionaries is unlikely to organize a very successful conference. Equally, those whose forte is administration will be essential members of the team, but a conference team full of administrators alone might not have the gift of making the event as powerful and inspiring as it could have been if there had been appropriate input from a visionary. A key job of the support members of the team is to stand in front of the speeding train that the visionary sometimes resembles, and say, 'Hang on, let's talk about how we can operationalize this.'
- **Bring in individuals with specific responsibility as and when they are needed.** There is no need to have the caterer in to discuss the planned topic for the conference, or to include the conference chair in discussions on the lunch menus. It can be useful to have short general meetings of the whole

team, so everyone can be updated quickly on the overall picture of how the planned conference is emerging, then to have scheduled sub-group meetings dealing with specific aspects such as catering, handbook production and so on, attended by those with the specific responsibilities, but with one member of the overall planning team in attendance, so that the strings can be pulled together in due course.

- **Organize a de-brief after the event.** Invite the planning group to a final meeting, for example over lunch, to give everyone a chance to compare notes on what worked and what didn't work, and why not. Such a de-brief can provide an invaluable baseline from which to begin the planning of your next event.

Leading a conference team

We have already looked at some of the key processes to be considered by a conference team. However, such a team normally needs some sort of leader. Leading the team that organizes a successful conference is very rewarding. However the role requires many skills, abilities and knowledge. Before agreeing to take on this role (if you have a choice!), you may want to consider the following suggestions and questions.

- **Ensure you feel comfortable in this role.** If not, invest in some staff development which can boost your confidence and abilities in areas you feel concerned about, such as financial planning or people management.
- **Have you already a track record in leading a planning team towards a successful conference?** If so, fine, but if not, look carefully at this section to see what you will need to be thinking about if you intend to be the principal player in putting together a conference.
- **Are there experienced people around you who you can bring into your team?** Even if you only recruit them to cover specific aspects, their experience can be invaluable, and can save you a lot of time and energy.
- **Embrace delegation.** As leader of the planning team, you may feel that you should be involved in every area, but beware – that way madness lies. You will also find that colleagues are much more willing to contribute if given full responsibility for organizing a particular aspect of the event, such as the development of the exhibition or compilation of the delegate pack.
- **What's in it for you personally?** Will the benefits of your taking a leading role in organizing the conference be sufficient to keep you going during the dark and difficult days which are bound to come up from time to time?
- **What's the worst that could happen to you personally?** How would it reflect on you if something were to go seriously wrong with the conference? Would the blame come to rest on your shoulders? Is it worth the risk? Do the potential benefits outweigh the risks?

- **Think carefully about what time you are likely to have available.** Be realistic about how long planning and leading a conference is actually going to take.
- **Schedule in time in your diary well in advance.** You'll need to include time for planning, administration, troubleshooting and dealing with contingencies as well as for the actual event. Organizing a conference is like an iceberg: the bits that you don't see actually make up the bulk of the endeavour.
- **What skills will you need to acquire?** For most people, leading the planning of their first major conference is a steep learning curve. If you spend time working out exactly where you will need to pick up new skills, you'll be able to do so much more efficiently. This book as a whole should help you to identify the most significant gaps in your existing experience and expertise, which you will need to bridge.
- **Will you have sufficient followers?** A leader can't work without other people who are willing and able to follow the lead. Are the people you will need to delegate things to willing to be led? Are they willing to be led by you in particular?
- **What will be your leadership approach?** Are you the sort of person who prefers to lead by example? Will you be the sort of leader willing to get your hands dirty? Will you not baulk at working on the production line, putting together delegate packs or stuffing envelopes for mail shots when such things need to be done quickly? Will you be able to find people at short notice to help out with urgent tasks?
- **What are your blind spots?** We all have them. Do you know about your 'unconscious uncompetences'? Of course you don't. But will you be looking for the important things you don't yet know you are not very good at, and finding ways to work round them as you discover them?
- **Right from the outset, start a highly organized system to manage your paperwork.** It is all too easy for the trivia to get missed unless your filing is first rate.
- **Clear your desk.** Ensure that you have no major activities in your diary in the weeks leading up to the event. Avoid having competing tasks which would make it difficult to dedicate your time to organizing the conference when this becomes the most important task on your agenda.
- **Build a personal conference planning file.** Or get one of your team to build one. This should include all the duties you have taken on yourself, all the places you need to go to, reminders and checklists about housekeeping, announcements and so on. This will be invaluable to you, and worth more than rubies if something should happen to prevent your attendance.
- **Build in to your budget the costs of help.** Save your sanity by budgeting in advance for a temp to help you with the last-minute administration. You should not be staying up until midnight on the evening before the conference to get the badges and signposting done.

- **Work out what your strengths are, and play to them.** If you are a visionary with poor finishing skills, use your talents to set the tone for the conference, and step well away from the detailed planning.
- **Have plans in place to cover your duties should something happen to you.** Make sure your team knows what they will do during the event if illness, accident or other problems prevent you from being there.

Developing your project plan

Your project plan is an essential tool which will help you and other members of the planning team keep abreast of all the parallel activities going on in the lead-up to your conference. The plan also forms a vital means of communicating changes in details. The form of the project plan is not material – you can choose to use an online planning tool or the back of an envelope (although the latter is not recommended!). But what is important is that the plan is kept up to date and available to all. In developing the plan, you should consider the following suggestions:

- **Start to plan as soon as is feasible.** As a rough rule of thumb you will want to start the planning process for respective types of event with at least the following timescales in mind:
  - institutional, local event: six months;
  - national: 12 months;
  - international: 18 months.
- **Ensure your plan covers all areas of the conference.** The plan will not be of much value if essential elements are missed out, and roles and responsibilities are not allocated. Get help to prepare an extensive overall checklist for your conference, and continue to update and refine this all the way through the planning stages.
- **Get hold of some past conference planning paperwork.** Even if the theme and style of those conferences were quite different from the one you are planning, you can learn a lot from the ways different people went about the task of planning their events. If your conference is one in a series, make particular efforts to get hold of the planning paperwork from previous events, and learn from the changes that needed to be made as the plans developed.
- **Put people into your plan.** It is essential that everyone can see where they fit into the overall picture. Whether you use names or role descriptors, make sure that everyone knows which parts of the plan will be down to them.
- **Use a Gantt chart.** This will explicitly show timelines and how different aspects of the conference relate and are contingent on one another.
- **Think about employing an online planning package if you are organizing a large event.** A possible package to consider is Microsoft Project. However

build in time to learn to use it first. You will not be able to use it effectively until you have gone up the associated learning curve. Once learnt, however, such packages can save you vast amounts of time – perhaps in connection with your next conference.

- **Keep the plan up to date.** Note developments and changes as soon as they appear, such as milestones reached and changes to the original scheme. An outdated plan often results in missed deadlines and duplication of effort.

- **Find a means to ensure that all members of the planning team can access the plan so they are aware of developments and changes.** There is no point your knowing what each person should be doing if he or she does not know it. If the plan is in hard copy, secure it to a wall where all can see it. If it is in electronic form, place it in a shared directory so that all who consult it see the latest version each time they open it. Alternatively, e-mail frequent updates to the team, making sure that each update bears the date, or a version number where it can easily be seen, so that past versions can be discarded.

- **Don't spend so long preparing the project plan that you neglect starting on the activities themselves.** It is tempting to try to develop a 'perfect' schedule, with coloured tabs and detailed notes, but some of the tasks that need long-term planning – such as booking the venue – might need to be undertaken early and quickly, long before other details of the plan are finalized.

- **Don't be afraid to change the plan.** A good plan is a flexible one. For example, if the conference turns out to be attracting twice the number of delegates originally envisaged, several aspects of your original plan will need updating.

Costing the event

Those who have run several successful conferences will tell you that getting the price right is critically important. They will also usually explain that costing events is a steep learning curve, especially for the first few events. In short, the danger is that you will end up running at a loss. Someone has to pay for this loss at the end of the day, and whoever this is, they are not likely to thank you for it (at best!). Making a profit is not usually a problem, of course. But getting the balance right is tricky, and involves juggling several quite different things at once. The following suggestions should help you to get this right – or at least to work out exactly what you need to be trying to juggle.

- **Do not confuse cost with price.** Costs are incurred, prices are charged. As a rule of thumb for your planning purposes, the delegate price you charge will reflect the costs incurred by you to organize the event. Remember that the total costs incurred by your delegates will include the event price you charge them, and other expenditure associated with their attendance at your event, such as their travel to the venue, subsistence *en route*, and so on.

- **Decide upon the financial basis on which you are running the conference.** For example, are you aiming to recover the costs? Is someone paying for the delegates to attend, or are they paying themselves, or is it likely to be a mixture? Are the delegates in a position where you could make a profit from them? Do you need to break even with the conference, or will someone guarantee you against ending up running at a loss?
- **Decide on the optimum number of delegates.** You will need to know this so you can work out how the fixed costs can be shared out.
- **Work out your fixed costs.** These are all the things you will need to take account of however many people attend (or how few), for example room hire, advertising, staff costs and equipment hire. The fixed costs will need to be divided among the number of delegates who actually pay to attend.
- **Prepare for the unexpected too.** Add a contingency to cover unplanned items such as price increases. Factor in at least 10 per cent of the total fixed costs as a contingency buffer, and don't forget to add VAT (Value Added Tax or its equivalent) to relevant costs.
- **Work out your variable costs.** These are all the things that vary according to the number of delegates who attend, for example accommodation costs, catering costs, delegate gifts, handbook and photocopying of handout materials.
- **Work out what the cost per delegate will be, depending on how many people register.** Look at costings for a depressingly low number of registrations, then for what you guess will be the likely number of delegates, and also for a best case scenario (for example, the maximum number which could be accommodated in the main lecture theatre, or at the conference dinner). You can then use these estimates of the cost per delegate to decide how you will fix the price for delegates, and to build in a suitable margin for profit or contingency as appropriate.
- **Consider the price of delegate places.** If you are going for cost recovery only this will be achieved by adding together the variable cost per person and the fixed cost divided by the anticipated number of delegates.
- **Err on the side of caution.** If you have to recover costs, you must ensure that the costs you incur are covered by the fees paid by the worst case scenario of number of delegates.
- **Consider different prices for different people.** For example, you may wish to offer a reduction for early bookings, a loyalty bonus for previous delegates rebooking, a 'member' discount, a discount for presenters, and so on.
- **Think about the effects of charging different prices for different people, however.** Will it cause some delegates to feel badly done by? Will it be difficult to administer? Will it cost more to administer than it saves?
- **You can only stay within your budget if you know how much your event is costing.** Event costing is not only about calculating prices and profit margins. Even where an organization is funded specifically to deliver free-to-user training events or conferences, a budget will either be allocated or need to be determined for each separate event.

- **Think sensitively about the profit margin.** If you want to make a profit, decide how big this should be. Pricing is a very delicate issue, and if you put the price too high you may deter potential delegates who think the event is too expensive. This will certainly be the case if you are too greedy.
- **Remember there's no such thing as a free lunch.** You need to include in your fixed costs how much you are spending on free or reduced-rate delegate places, for example for members of the organizing team and key presenters.
- **Will presenters be expected to attend as paying delegates or will you be paying them?** This will depend on the type of event you are running, but whatever you decide, make the decision early and factor in the costs or income accordingly. Remember that some presenters may not be willing to take part at full price, especially if they are paying for the event from their own pockets, and you could lose some key contributions if they are put off by the price.
- **Staff time is not a free resource.** Whether or not to include staff time in your calculations is a topic for considerable debate. If your organization exists solely to deliver events and is grant-funded to do so, you may feel that running events is what your staff are paid to do, and therefore staff time does not need to be included in your sums. In almost all other circumstances, however, you need to know how much staff time will be required and how much it is costing. You may need to justify staff expenditure to senior colleagues, or you may be bidding for additional staff resources specifically for the event. If your organization is self-funding, in either the commercial or not-for-profit sectors, your major events may be one of the principal income streams by which you support the organization's infrastructure. Whether you pass the cost on to delegates, or secure the funding from sponsors, you need to know how much staff time is costing – and remember, everything takes longer than you might think.
- **Outsourcing.** This involves considerable planning and budgeting. However, it can be cost-effective in appropriate circumstances to outsource one or more of a range of aspects of the preparation and implementation of a conference or event. Event management companies operate on just such a basis. You need to make a careful choice if you decide to use such a company, and select one that has exactly the right sort of experience for the nature of the conference you are planning. Outsourcing is justified when the cost of buying in expertise is recouped in terms of the time and energy saved by doing so, and when the overall quality of the final event is enhanced significantly, and recruitment and attendance are improved to the extent that the costs of outsourcing are recovered well.

Marketing

Marketing starts when you decide what event you are offering, why, and for which audience, where and when. Marketing is big business! Yet many people end up taking their first steps into marketing in contexts such as planning and organizing a conference. They can find themselves thrown into the huge field of marketing at the deep end. The following suggestions should help you to put the most relevant principles of good marketing to work for you and your conference.

- **Marketing is not the same as promotion or sales.** Often the terms are used interchangeably, but you will find it more helpful to think of promotion and sales as distinct activities or phases in your event planning process, underpinned by a marketing strategy which starts with offering the right event at the right time to meet an identified need.
- **Marketing is about building a relationship and rapport with your potential customers.** If you demonstrate that you listen to feedback and respond to demand, your potential delegates are more likely to identify with your organization and your events. For example, if you use phrases like 'to improve the way we meet your needs', 'in response to feedback received last time', 'we're offering this event to address a training need identified in the 2003 member survey' you demonstrate that your events are designed for the delegate's benefit.
- **Marketing starts with 'Why?'** There need to be good reasons for putting on your event in the first place, especially if it is a one-off event, or the first in an intended series of events. These reasons need to appeal to the people you want to participate – they need good reasons for turning up and taking part.
- **Marketing continues with 'What?'** You must have something to offer to the market place. That might seem straightforward enough if you are planning an event or a conference, but what kind of event exactly is it going to be? You need to be really clear in your own mind what sort of event it will be, for you to be able to start marketing it really effectively.
- **Marketing continues with 'For whom?'** If your event has been planned with a specific audience and purpose in mind, to meet an identified need, you have essentially already determined your market and your product. Make sure you know who your event is aimed at, and what benefit they will derive from attending.
- **Marketing may involve 'Where?'** If the location of your conference is in your control, why is the particular location found to be the best? Why will this choice of venue be good for those who attend? If you have identified good responses to these questions, hang on to them and make sure that your potential delegates know about them from your conference literature.

- **Marketing also involves 'When?'** Is the time right for this conference or event? Why is this a good time for it? Why is this the ideal time for it? If you already have good answers to these questions, you are well on your way to marketing your choice of time to the intended audience.
- **Know your stakeholders.** Who has an interest in the success of your event? Your delegates will have particular expectations but so too will your sponsors, your organization, exhibitors, the media, your staff, the venue and your suppliers. Each of these groups will expect different information from you, to reassure them that their investment is secure, that the event will reflect well on those associated with it, that bills will be paid, or that the event will provide interesting information or stories. Being aware of stakeholder interests in advance will mean you can plan to keep them appropriately briefed without having to take valuable time to respond to *ad hoc* requests for information when you are busy with the event administration.
- **Know the competition.** What other conferences and workshops already attract your intended audience? When and where do the events take place, and how much do they cost? Before you define your event and publicize it, make sure you are not going into head-to-head competition with other suppliers or providers. Identify what is unique about your event and build on this competitive advantage to define your event, so you can promote it in a targeted way.
- **Find out what events potential delegates want.** Plan events which meet identified needs rather than 'It just seems like a good idea.' Your idea may be really great and prove very popular, but you are taking a huge risk if the need for the specific event has not been identified from surveys and feedback from your intended audience.
- **Keep your colleagues happy.** Good marketing will involve your internal stakeholders, so keep them informed. Let them know well in advance about any assistance you might require or disruption you may cause. There will be things you need to do to satisfy finance colleagues and auditors, like making sure bookings from companies, universities or other organizations are accompanied by purchase orders, so make sure you consult specialists within your own organization. You should be continually mindful of the impact your event will have on others in your organization.
- **Effective marketing relies on effective infrastructure.** The financial processing and IT infrastructure behind your organization are crucial to positive customer perceptions, and are therefore part of the marketing strategy, so get specialist colleagues on side early. Consult your internal experts from the beginning. Make them aware of your event requirements, and be mindful of theirs.
- **Find marketeers.** Most organizations already contain people who have experience of at least some aspects of marketing. Some of your colleagues may engage in marketing outside their normal spheres of activity, for example in connection with leisure pursuits. Some may have been involved in

marketing in a previous post. Such people can be sources of wisdom and even inspiration, so make sure that they know that their suggestions will be welcomed, and if they are particularly keen and experienced, find ways of building them into the conference planning process. Show them your appreciation, too.

Promoting your event

This is very much a matter of getting your wording right. Your promotional material needs to say the right things about your conference, to the right people, and in the most appropriate way. The following suggestions should help you to fine-tune your promotional material, so that as far as possible the right people end up as your delegates.

- **Match the tone and style of your promotional material to the target audience, and to the purpose of your event.** Is your conference or workshop being run as an internal or external event? Will delegates attend your event on a voluntary or compulsory basis? If there is something mandatory about taking part in the event, you need to be sensitive in how you persuade people to attend. Equally if you want potential delegates to perceive your event as professional and valuable, make sure you communicate in a professional manner. If your target audience is predominantly from a particular subject-focused culture, use terminology they will find familiar and interesting.
- **Promote your event to the right audience.** If you have planned your event in response to identifiable demand and focused the content and format towards a clearly defined audience, your promotional effort can focus on telling such people about your event. In such cases, your promotional material can be quite specific to this identified target audience, so that they immediately feel that this is the right event for them to attend.
- **Be stylish.** Develop a logo or style to characterize your promotional material. This will help to identify your particular event, and to distinguish it from others. You may already be starting off with an institutional or organizational logo, but you could consider running this alongside a new logo specifically relating to your conference. You can also carry through the design for use in the delegate information pack, and venue signage at the event itself.
- **Don't promise too much.** In the excitement of planning a conference or event, it is quite easy to get carried away with your own enthusiasm, and that of fellow members of the planning team. The danger then is raising people's expectations too high when they see the publicity materials. It is better if their expectations are reasonable and realistic, and that they are pleasantly surprised by the quality of your event, than the other way round.
- **Anticipate what people need to know.** There are significant demands on people's time and a huge range of workshops, conferences, seminars and

exhibitions from which to choose. Make sure you make their choice of your event easy by clearly stating the theme or topic, who the event is aimed at, what prior knowledge or experience is required or expected, when and where the event is taking place, and how much it will cost. Remember that even if your event seems cheaply priced, the cost to the delegate includes time away from work, travel time and expense.

- **Make it easy for the right people to see that your event is ideal for them.** If potential delegates can see quickly that the event is relevant to them, they are more likely to proceed with a booking without laboriously looking elsewhere. Spelling out the intended target audiences carefully can help.

- **Don't be afraid of people rejecting your event.** If the event is not right for people reading your promotional materials, they need to be able to decide swiftly to reject it, without wasting their time or yours. There is little, if any, benefit in people attending an event that is wrong for them, especially if the experience alienates them so they reject your events out of hand in the future.

- **Don't end up attracting the wrong people.** If the publicity material is too broadly focused, you may end up with a significant number of delegates who simply don't get what they feel they had been led to expect from your event. It only takes a relatively small proportion of dissatisfied delegates to plunge a whole conference into a downward spiral.

- **Provide information early.** Time pressure is one of the principal reasons for people not attending conferences and training events. If you know your potential delegates have heavy demands on their time (and who doesn't?) make sure your date is in their diary early. This is especially important if your event is aimed at senior colleagues or those whose work patterns may be unpredictable.

- **Word of mouth is the most powerful promotional tool.** This links to the notion of marketing being about building relationships. If your delegates go away from one of your events satisfied that it has been time and money well spent, they will recommend you to others.

- **Decide how you are going to tell people about your event – electronic or hard copy.** There is an immediacy to direct electronic communications like e-mail, and there is certainly convenience in being able to mount large amounts of information cost-effectively on a Web site. That said, many people are still reluctant to rely entirely on virtual communication, especially if they are parting with money. Understanding your audience will help with the decision. If you are targeting a technically sophisticated group you may safely communicate through cyberspace. Otherwise consider a hybrid of attention-grabbing fliers with more information available online, or on request. Make sure your preferred medium, whatever you choose, is accessible to a wide variety of individuals, including those with particular mobility or sensory requirements.

- **Make sure delegates know what they are booking for.** You will avoid a great deal of misunderstanding and bad feeling if you are very clear about what is – and is not – included in the delegate package. Do not assume everyone has the same understanding of 'student accommodation', for example. Spell out if it has shared bathroom facilities and no television. Be clear which meals, social activities and workshops are included, and what extras are available. Remember that people really do need to know precise start and finish times, so they can make themselves available and organize travel. Your delegates will also need to know if there are any inherent accessibility issues with the venue, for example if you are using a large campus with long walks between residences and conference rooms, or an historic venue with limited facilities, or a city centre location with limited parking, and so on.

- **Make the booking process as easy as possible.** You don't want to spend excessive amounts of time correcting booking errors, and you don't want your delegates to arrive at the event already frustrated by overly complicated booking arrangements. There is no second chance to make a good first impression, and those first few minutes spent booking the conference are important in setting the mood for many delegates. Plan for it. You may need to provide step-by-step guidance to help delegates complete the booking form accurately. For example if a membership number is required for a discount, tell them what format the number is in and where they can find it. Online booking processes can be particularly good for validating each step of the booking process so incorrect entries cannot be made, but you will need to liaise closely with IT specialists and allow plenty of time for development and testing of such a programme. That said, the benefits of presenting a modern image and saving time may make the investment worthwhile.

- **Satisfy your legal obligations relating to data-protection.** You cannot hold information electronically or in hard copy without the explicit consent of the data subject. That means you cannot even hold the contact details for a delegate unless they have given informed consent to your doing so. Make sure the booking form tells the customer what information you are holding, in what format and for what purpose. For example, include wording such as, 'The information supplied by you on this form will be held in electronic and paper format for the purposes of administering the event.'

- **Satisfy other legal obligations.** For example, in the UK you will need to accommodate the requirements of the Disability Discrimination Act and the Special Educational Needs and Disability Act. In providing any goods or services the law requires you to anticipate special needs and ensure equality of experience for all. You need to be able to make 'reasonable adjustments' to meet the needs of all delegates. It is no longer adequate to rely on disclosure of individual needs by the attendees. That said, it is far easier for event organizers to anticipate needs if they invite delegates to tell them about their requirements in advance.

Sponsorship

You may not need sponsorship, of course. Depending upon what kind of event you are planning, sponsorship could be appropriate – or quite inappropriate. If you have never been involved in seeking sponsorship and negotiating with sponsors, you may feel that it is a strange new world you are stepping into. Where appropriate, however, sponsorship can add value to your event. It can make some things possible which would not otherwise have been an option. It can make your event more attractive to delegates. It can keep the price down, or it can move the quality of the event up. The following suggestions should help you to make up your mind whether or not to chase after some sponsorship, and if so, how to go about it.

- **Consider whether sponsorship is worth seeking.** The time spent contacting potential sponsors may outweigh the potential benefits. It may in the end cost you more in staff time, especially if you have little success in persuading people to give you money.
- **Ask around.** Talk to people who have organized similar events, possibly events you have attended yourself. It is best to talk to people who have already attracted the sort of delegates you wish to attract to your own event, as they will know what sorts of sponsors might be most likely to be interested in a similar target audience for their sponsorship.
- **Consider whether sponsorship is appropriate to your event.** There may be a political or commercial dimension which means you may not wish to be under an obligation to a potential sponsor. It is also the case that sponsorship by certain companies or organizations may alienate potential delegates or strategic stakeholders.
- **Think about what's in it for the sponsor.** The sponsor may have expectations about what they are 'buying' when giving you sponsorship. It is best to clarify up front what you are asking and what you are offering. Developing a standard tariff for sponsorship may save you time and uncomfortable negotiations. You may consider offering co-badging, exhibition space, mutual advertising, or similar benefits for the sponsor.
- **Find out what potential sponsors would like back from you.** Ask them (sensitively, of course) why they are interested in being sponsors for your particular event. Ask them what it is about the sort of people who are likely to be involved in your event that interests them.
- **Be creative in seeking sponsors if this is what you decide to do.** You will be amazed what people will give you if you ask them, as many companies have budgets for this kind of thing. Don't hesitate to ask – you won't be given anything if you don't ask!
- **Don't take it personally if a potential sponsor says no.** There are many factors that influence a potential sponsor, very few of which will be anything

to do with you or your event. The sponsor's own business priorities, an existing marketing strategy, existing sponsorship commitments or changing adverse economic conditions will all impact on their ability to respond positively to your request.

- **Don't give up too soon.** If a potential sponsor says 'no' to your initial suggestions regarding what it might be willing to do to sponsor your event, keep the channels of communication open. For example, bounce the response back, and ask if the organization itself has any suggestions about alternative ways it might be interested in backing your event. You could even ask if it happens to know of any similar sources of sponsorship. The idea of a competitor stepping into the breach sometimes encourages organizations to give some backing themselves.
- **Seek sponsorship early.** Organizations tend to have set budgets for sponsorship which are often committed a long time ahead. No matter how worthy your cause, if they have committed their budget for the year ahead already they will not be able to support you. If a sponsor has already spent such a budget, it can still be worth asking it now whether they might be interested in your next-but-one event.
- **Consider seeking sponsorship in kind.** Many organizations won't be able to give you hard cash but could give you reductions on their goods and services, such as venue hire, equipment hire, delegate bags, and other goods or services.
- **Remember to say thank you publicly to your sponsors.** The pay-off for sponsors comes in public recognition, so you should make sure they get mentioned in the conference literature, the opening or closing comments, at receptions, and wherever it is appropriate to make your thanks to them public.
- **Remember to say thank you privately as well.** After your event has been successful, it is well worth the time spent to write an individual 'thank you' letter to each sponsor. It doesn't cost much to do so, it may well be much appreciated by them, and indeed it may keep the door open for future sponsorship from them.
- **Be sensitive to your sponsors' competitive environment.** For example, it might not be wise to invite two publishers who compete directly with each other to sponsor the same aspects of your event. It may be better to get one to sponsor a reception and another to put its logo on your bags at a price.
- **Be hard-nosed about what you offer reciprocally for their sponsorship.** Don't feel you have to bend over backwards to emblazon their logo everywhere if their financial input is modest. Be very clear about what you are prepared to trade for the cash or goods the sponsor offers.

5 Detailed planning

Several aspects of planning already discussed in the previous sections of this book have gone into considerable detail. However, in the sections which follow, we get down even further into the hour-to-hour and minute-to-minute planning of a conference or event. In particular, this section of the book addresses:

- timetable overview;
- planning for contingencies;
- social programme;
- delegate (delicate?) issues;
- food for thought;
- designing your handbook, and session options;
- administration: time and motion.

However, most of these aspects could be things that in your context need to be considered during early planning too. Moreover, many of these need to be continuously fine-tuned and adjusted during the event as well as before it.

Whatever your own context, we trust that in this section you will find many suggestions that will help you to maximize the effectiveness of various aspects of your conference or event – and equally will help you to avoid many of the things which might otherwise have gone wrong.

Timetable overview

The timetable is one of the most useful planning tools. Start to draw your timetable up early – if only in draft form – to get a good idea of the shape and scope of the event. Putting concrete dates and times against the various inputs and elements will help your team share the same view of the event, and encourage all to believe it is really going to happen! The following suggestions should help you in developing the timetable for your event.

- **Start at an appropriate time to suit the majority of your target audience.** A national or regional event in the UK for example should start at a time – perhaps 10.30 or 11 am – which will give participants from a reasonable distance the chance to travel there on the day and to arrive in time for the start. In order to help the minority whose travelling time will take longer, provide them with opportunity for pre-conference accommodation so they can choose to be there at the start if they wish. An in-house event and the second or third days of a residential conference can probably be started early – at 9–9.30 am – as all participants are likely to be either on-site or fairly local.

- **Provide sufficient time for people to register.** Participants do not like arriving in order to join a mile-long queue. They do appreciate this time to delve into their pack (which will avoid much annoying rustling at the start of the plenary sessions), network with colleagues, have a preliminary look at the exhibition – and be plied with coffee.

- **Begin the day formally with an introduction and welcome from the chair.** This provides an opportunity for individuals to focus, be informed and be 'warmed up' for the first keynote. It also allows a little time for slippage if your first speaker happens to be late – or indeed for him or her to catch breath and tune in to the venue. It is also less embarrassing for delegates arriving late due to traffic chaos to slip in during the introductions, than to enter at just that instant where the opening keynoter has got the whole assembled audience so intent that a pin could be heard dropping.

- **Ensure appropriate lengths of time are provided for all sessions.** Participants will feel frustrated if there are no opportunities to question the keynotes, participate fully in workshops and contribute to discussions. But don't provide too much time – only a few minutes' boredom can spoil the overall impression of what had been feeling like an interesting session. It is better to stop a discussion some time before it fizzles out, than to endure the closing minutes with silences punctuated by, 'Has anyone got just one more question now please?'

- **Provide sufficient time for individuals to move between sessions.** Neither participants nor presenters will relish having to run between sessions, or attend sessions that are constantly interrupted during the first 10 minutes as panting participants arrive or – worse – leave early in order to arrive on time for their next session. It can be useful to plan in 10-minute breaks between the end of one session and the start of the next, except where a longer break will be there anyway for refreshments or lunch.

- **Provide sufficient breaks.** Even if all of the participants are scheduled to be in the same room for three successive sessions, plan in a break or two. People sitting still for too long at a time become bored and irritable – let alone the risk of deep vein thrombosis! Comfort breaks will give participants the opportunity to move about, network with colleagues, pay essential visits and be plied with yet more coffee.

- **Ensure adequate refreshments.** Refreshments by way of coffee, tea and water will facilitate concentration and stimulate discussion. Their provision does not necessarily always mean a break in the programme: coffee can be provided in breakout rooms at the start of seminar or discussion sessions. This device will not only encourage participants to move swiftly to these sessions in search of their cups, but can also stimulate discussion. Similarly, water jugs or coolers together with plenty of disposable cups will keep participants in their sessions rather than leaving early in search of hydration.

- **Provide a concluding plenary session.** Although many participants may not choose to attend such a session, the majority prefer a conference to be brought to an end in this way. It provides opportunities for final discussions, thanks, and for intimation of the details of the next conference to be provided.
- **Avoid ending with a whimper.** Avoid the awful spectacle of the room emptying before your eyes as presenters and participants alike run out of the room as their taxis, trains, planes, children beckon. Finish a little early by all means, but absolutely never over-run at the final session. Those who want to continue to talk can remain behind for a while, or continue their discussion outside the main plenary room if they wish.

Planning for contingencies

A key part of planning for events and conferences is ensuring that you are not wrong-footed when things go wrong (as they inevitably will from time to time, even if you have planned for just about everything). You cannot of course predict everything that could possibly go wrong, but in envisaging the worst, our experience tells us that you can come up with a range of generic solutions to issues that might arise, and these are likely to help you work your way out of even the worst situations that fate can throw at you. We start this section with some general suggestions about contingency planning, then we outline some of the most common problems that arise, with some advice on how to address them.

- **Expect the unexpected.** The point of contingency planning is to have strategies for coping with unplanned eventualities. Thinking carefully about what might go wrong should not be seen as 'tempting fate'.
- **It's only scary if you haven't thought of it.** Contingency planning is the comfort blanket of event management. You may scare your team witless by brainstorming the worst things that could go wrong before or during your event, but having logged your worst fears, you and your team can confront them head-on and make sensible judgements about how likely it is that the nightmares will actually happen, and if they did, how devastating they would actually be. Going the next step and knowing what you would do to mitigate the impact is actually very reassuring.
- **Do it early.** Your earliest contingency planning should be mostly concerned with administrative difficulties – knowing what you will do if you don't get

enough bookings, how you will cope if the IT doesn't work, how you will handle unexpected staff shortages through sickness and the like.

- **Do it again.** Keep reviewing your contingency plans at appropriate points in the run-up to your event. What will you do if a confirmed keynote pulls out, or the venue notifies you of unexpected building work? These are the sorts of thing that crop up once you are past the point of no return, but you still have time to do something about them. We have offered more detailed suggestions about specific scenarios below, but keep thinking of the particular contingencies that could be unique to your event.

- **And again just before the event starts.** You don't want to overdo it and have your team collapse in a state of high anxiety, but you might want to have a really off-the-wall contingency brainstorm very near to the event, to think about emergencies and crises that might occur during the event.

- **The more bizarre the problem, the more creative the solution.** Don't be afraid of using real brainstorming for your contingency planning, and avoid dismissing contributions as too bizarre. Relieve tension, have some fun, and laugh at the idea that you might have to deal with a bear attack at a conference in a UK city, but still determine who would take what action in the event of such an occurrence. You may not get the bear but you could get a feral dog, an escaped 'exotic' pet or an aggressive gatecrasher, and you will know what to do. Below are more detailed suggestions for specific possible contingencies, but don't forget to plan similar actions for the sorts of things which may be more likely for your particular event.

- **Key speakers fail to turn up or are taken ill during the event.** It is a good idea to plan what to do if a speaker is unable to fulfil his or her commitments. If the input is fairly small, the programme for most events is usually full enough to allow you to take up a bit of slack, but if the input is a major one, you will need to assess the extent to which you can offer an alternative, or whether you will need to cancel the event outright. If the speaker is an internationally-renowned figure who is likely to be the main draw at your event, you will need to be prepared for extreme delegate disappointment which they are likely to take out on you, whether or not the problem is one over which you have any control. If the event is one for which delegates have paid, you will need to be prepared for them asking for their money back. For this, and many other reasons, it is a good idea to take out both public liability and event insurance for such events. For short inputs, it is an excellent idea to have someone on stand-by to step in if things go wrong, but this may not be feasible.

- **Insufficient delegates book for the event.** This should not be a problem if you have done the right kind of market research prior to advertising the event, and if you have set your prices appropriately to cover all fixed costs, based on a pessimistic estimate of numbers likely to attend, but of course it happens sometimes. It is best not to commit yourself to details such as contracts with venues until you can be reasonably certain you can recruit sufficient numbers to make the event viable. In some cases, particularly with not-for-profit organizations and charitable bodies, it may be possible to get an external body to provide a guarantee against loss for events. If you do end up with an event with depressingly low numbers of delegates booking, you will need to do some hard thinking about how much it will cost you (both financially and in PR terms) to cancel the event, and in some cases, bite the bullet and do so. Running a very small event, perhaps rebadged as an expert seminar, might in some cases be less damaging than cancelling outright, however.

- **Delegates fail to turn up.** This is a particularly common occurrence when events are offered free. Delegates may book for the event, but drop out often at the last minute, and perhaps without warning if something else turns up. With free events, it may help to send an e-mail reminder to delegates immediately before the event, asking for confirmation of attendance so that catering numbers can be adjusted at the last minute if necessary. Within some organizations, free events are free to those who turn up, but a non-attendance charge is levied on people who booked but did not attend. This improves attendance, and saves wastage of catering where provided. With paid-for events, obviously the organizers need to ensure that drop-outs do not cause financial problems for the event, by setting prices to ensure that there are financial penalties for pulling out of attendance at a stage when it is too late to recruit replacements or cancel the event.

- **One of the speakers behaves inappropriately.** Just occasionally event organizers can be embarrassed by one of their speakers behaving in a racist, sexist or homophobic manner. It is almost impossible to prevent this entirely, although clear guidelines for speakers and presenters being provided at the outset on such issues can help minimize the possibility, and will make it less possible for the event organizers to be blamed if things do go wrong. As alcohol is sometimes a factor in such behaviour, it is possibly best not to ply after-dinner speakers, for example, with too much wine over dinner prior to their public speaking. Inappropriate speaker behaviour usually comes as a surprise, but quite often the particular kind of behaviour turns out to have been encountered before by those who know the individuals concerned. It can be useful discreetly to check out whether there is any known history associated with people you are considering inviting to be key speakers at your event.

- **A delegate behaves inappropriately.** Again, nothing you can do will make this contingency completely avoidable, so you will need to have plans in place to limit the damage, whether it is actual damage or a public relations issue. Sometimes, simply having a quiet word with the person causing offence may be sufficient. In other cases you may have to ask the delegate to leave. In the most serious cases, a more interventionist approach might be necessary, up to and including having the delegate removed by police or security staff. There is a balance to be struck between being seen as organizers not to tolerate inappropriate behaviour and making too much of a fuss. Delegates will need to be reassured that you are taking the matter sufficiently seriously but not going completely over the top.

- **Something goes badly wrong with the venue before the event starts.** This might include a fire at the venue or an over-run of refurbishment activities that should have been completed prior to your event. In some academic venues, a not uncommon problem is double-booking, especially where normal users did not realize the need for them to indicate their plans to use classrooms and other facilities outside term time. Where possible, it is advisable at least to have explored alternative venues where the event could be relocated at short notice. Where the fault lies clearly with the venue owner/booker, then it will have a responsibility to put the matter right. It is worthwhile to check contracts carefully with venues in advance to clarify where responsibility lies, and particularly where financial penalties fall when things go wrong. As indicated earlier, appropriate event insurance is always a good idea as a fallback.
- **A major national event coincides with your event.** Examples of this kind of thing include royal funerals and home matches in the late rounds of the football World Cup. You would be well advised to check with delegates what the majority want you to do (reschedule sessions, provide media coverage on large television screens in a different room, carry on as normal, cancel the event) and try to satisfy them as far as possible within your own organizational and budgetary limits. Be aware, though, that you will never be able to make everyone happy.
- **There is a major health problem during your event.** If one of your delegates contracts serious food-related problems or a highly contagious disease, you may be faced with a major issue. Planning in advance for such contingencies is essential. For example, ensure that you have available contact details for appropriate health professionals from whom to take advice on a major outbreak.
- **Someone is seriously ill.** The venue managers have a responsibility to provide you with information for use in an emergency. In any case, you will need to give all event staff a checklist in advance which contains local doctors' phone numbers and the location of the most appropriate hospital casualty department. If you have a trained first-aider on the conference team or at the event venue, that person will be well placed to advise on immediate action to be taken in the case of a medical emergency. A basic first aid kit can be helpful, but you should be careful about letting untrained staff offer advice or medication. It is good practice to ask delegates in advance if they have medical conditions about which it would be helpful to advise you, so you can, for example, have raisins available for diabetics who need something to help them through to the next meal.
- **The food provided for delegates is really unsatisfactory.** You may be surprised how much you find out about the catering provision at a conference

– or even a one-day event – only after the whole thing is over. Evaluation data usually gives you a lot of information about the provision, timing, quality and other aspects of refreshments. The most important thing is to check out continuously whether the catering is being found to be satisfactory or better. At least that way you have the chance to intervene and try to improve things if they are not going well. We have separate suggestions about catering, and also a case study about unsatisfactory catering, elsewhere in the book.

- **Timings of the event are badly thrown by delays to food service caused by queuing.** This ought not to happen if you have checked out the venue well in advance, discussed your requirements with the catering manager, built some slack into your programme and made reasonable estimates of how long things will take, but in actuality it often does happen, especially if there is slippage in the timetable or if the venue's caterers are over-optimistic about how quickly they can serve food.

- **There is a major transport problem affecting delegates' ability to come to or return from the event.** In the UK, for example, railway strikes and problems associated with adverse weather may interfere with planned transportation. Depending on the venue – and the season – it could be worth investigating whether you can take out some kind of insurance against the consequences of such events, as you are hardly likely to be able to get delegates to pay for the event if they could not get to it.

- **There are significant IT problems at the event.** It is useful to check out where you could hire in equipment locally at short notice. Most hotel chains use equipment companies for their own conferences and events. It might be expensive to hire in a couple of data projectors at short notice, but it could make all the difference to your conference if your keynotes would have been bereft without them, after your own equipment had let you down.

Social programme

Most events that last two or more days include a social dimension. Probably the most usual event is a conference dinner, but it can be really useful to think through what else you might wish to provide, particularly if there is more than one evening when delegates will be around. At large events, it can be useful to have at least some choices available to delegates (and any people accompanying them to the conference). The following suggestions may help you decide to what extent you should develop such a programme.

- **Aim to provide something for everyone.** If you plan to have a variety of social activities to provide choice for your delegates, make sure you have really offered something for all tastes. Planning a social programme is not the time to indulge your own entertainment preferences. Refer to feedback from previous events, take recommendations from locals and the venue team, canvas informal opinion.

- **Think about outsourcing the social programme.** In making the decision to have a varied social programme, you commit significant human and financial resources, and invite challenges as delegates choose more than one, change their minds and want to pair up with old acquaintances. You may consider outsourcing this aspect of your event to take advantage of local knowledge, expertise and agency purchasing power, as well as the attractive aspect of negotiating a price with your chosen agency and then letting them get on with it.

- **One size fits all?** Of course it doesn't; it just means that if you decide to provide one social option for all your delegates, you will have to make compromises and play it safe. When you are entertaining several hundred delegates is not the time to get overly adventurous.

- **Time, motion and money.** Notwithstanding the points about playing it safe, the social programme is a bit of fun to offset the intensive hard work of a residential event, so you might want to push the boat out a bit. Beware! Cost the social programme very, very carefully. Be very clear about how much you are paying per head for each activity, or if there is a flat rate regardless of numbers. Don't forget to factor in VAT. Check with social venues if there is room or equipment hire as well as a per head charge. Think about whether you will need a public address system, and include it in the costings. Know how long it will take to get all your delegates organized or grouped appropriately, and how you will transport them to the venue(s).

- **To everything there is a season.** Choose a venue with built-in facilities for a winter event, where provision of a health club or swimming pool may be much appreciated by delegates. For summer events consider locations where walking tour trails could be a pre-dinner option for delegates who wish for some local sightseeing and fresh air. Have fallback alternatives, however, in case of inclement weather.

- **Work hard, play hard.** Delegates and staff work very hard at academic conferences and will want to relax and unwind. It's probably best to impose a 'dry ship' policy on your core team at the event, and reward their work and abstinence with a party or outing after the event. Without wanting to cast aspersions on the delegate community, it's worth remembering that being away from home can lead to uncharacteristic behaviour amongst delegates, and it's important to be able to respond to challenging situations at your event.

- **Balance the booze.** As mentioned elsewhere, alcohol can play a significant part in behaviour difficulties. Decide how much (if of course any) you will provide at a particular event, and make appropriate arrangements for delegates to purchase more themselves. Copious free alcohol is more likely to result in problems, whereas personal budgets may be a self-regulating and limiting factor, reducing the likelihood of excessive consumption. In any event have a policy on how you will handle any difficulties, and make sure your team is briefed – and supported if things get out of hand.

Making a crisis out of a drama

What happened?

In 2000 we were lucky enough to secure a limited number of tickets to a unique theatrical production, never previously performed in that way or place, and not expected ever to be repeated – a truly once in a lifetime opportunity. The 30 tickets were offered to delegates at cost on a first come, first served basis – and sold like hot cakes.

Two delegates left a message with a conference steward that they would prefer to meet the group at the performance venue, and were assured that the tickets would be brought to them.

On the evening of the social programme, of which the drama trip was just one of six options, 250 delegates gathered in the foyer to be marshalled and sent their separate ways. Two drama tickets remained unclaimed, so not wanting to waste them or delay the party, the stewards handed them to two random delegates and the group departed for the performance.

About half an hour later two distressed delegates returned to the venue wanting to know where their tickets were, why their tickets hadn't been brought to them as promised, and why hadn't they been allowed into the performance. They had left a message at the conference desk saying that they would meet the party at the event venue, but this was never passed on.

What did we do?

We listened. Once the tickets had been given away there was no immediate action that could be taken, but a sympathetic listening ear went some way to reassuring the delegates that their situation was being taken seriously. That is not to say they were any less angry or upset!

We acknowledged our mistake. When nothing can apparently put a situation right you don't make it better by pretending it isn't a problem.

We took appropriate remedial action. The next day we sent a steward to queue for returned tickets. We were lucky and secured a pair of good seats for the evening performance.

What did we learn and what could we have done differently?

We learnt to tighten the message arrangements. The poor communication mechanisms that resulted in an important message not reaching anybody who could take the appropriate action caused huge distress, inconvenience and expense.

We clarified who in the team could and could not approve changes in arrangements. A steward confronted with the request to take the tickets to the performance could have said that wasn't possible, or could have found a more senior member of the team to deal with the request.

We made sure there would be a member of the event team left behind to deal with unexpected situations.

We improved the arrangements for the social programme, ensuring the muster takes place in a large enough space with plenty of time.

We ensured that all members of the team would be briefed about appropriate responses to distressed behaviour from delegates.

Delegate (delicate?) issues

There's no second chance to make a good first impression. This is particularly true of conferences. It's 'make or break': that first impression is generated in the first few minutes your delegates spend at your conference. Extensive research has however revealed that people arriving at a conference are very likely to be afflicted by a particular condition, which is discussed in the suggestions below:

- **Be prepared for CADS: conference acquired dependency syndrome.** (Examples follow after this section.) How is it that professional people, independently living busy and demanding lives, who have satisfactorily found their way to your event unaided, perhaps from around the world, become totally dependent on your conference team for every detail of their survival once they have registered at the event? The answer is simple. Regardless of the number of events attended over many years and in a variety of international locations, each separate event is a unique combination of time, place, content and people. This leads to what we call CADS, which manifests itself in a number of delegate behaviours ranging from the helpless to the aggressive. Recognize the causes and the symptoms to avoid delegate dissatisfaction.
- **Stepping into a strange, new, elaborately-organized world?** Even the most experienced delegates will feel disorientated on arrival at your event. It's hardly surprising – a conference team will frequently cover the venue signage

with its own posters, erect notice boards, use teaching rooms for exhibitions or social events, construct elaborate staging, and at the very least will plaster the venue with its logo and promotional materials, so even a familiar building is transformed into something different. A delegate may arrive expecting to see a number of familiar faces among the attendees, but among the familiar will be a host of new people. The timetable, housekeeping arrangements, catering and social programme will be specific to the event.

- **Strangers are friends you haven't met yet.** Make it possible for people to network with new contacts. During the early part of any event get people talking to delegates they haven't met or worked with before. Breaking the interpersonal barriers early will be an excellent way of curing CADS, and will make the conference activity productive quickly. It can really help to have opening keynotes that build in some element of interpersonal activity.
- **Cronies are friends you already know.** Make sure you give delegates an opportunity to catch up with old colleagues. Simply having plenty of seating in sight of the registration table can help, so that people looking out for old acquaintances have somewhere comfortable to wait and watch, till their friends turn up to book in.
- **Make the venue your own.** Create an identity for your event and the venue, so delegates can relate to it and feel comfortable within the event environment. Make sure the venue's essential signs to toilets, dining halls, halls of residence and so on are still visible, but reinforce them with your own event signage, which indicates areas your event is using and clearly identifies the usage by your event. Delegates suffering from CADS get lost easily, so you cannot have too much signage. If you developed a logo specifically for the conference, and used this on all the promotional materials and joining instructions, it can be useful to make the logo prominent on your event signage, as by then delegates will (even subconsciously) be associating the logo with the event.
- **There's no going back.** Even people who have recovered from CADS suffer from this. You have signposted the routes to everywhere and are pleased with yourself. But how do you get back to square one from the toilets, or from the dining areas, or from the plenary venue, or most particularly from Syndicate Room 5 which was a long way to get to in the first place? Some delegates booked in quite normally, but were never found again. They couldn't follow the reverse instructions, and joined another smaller, easier conference they happened to bump into. Could you find your way back easily from all the main rooms and facilities? It doesn't take long to add (preferably in a separate unique colour) some signs pointing back to the reception desk, or whatever point is going to be the best place to return to 'base' during the conference: for example the location of signing-in sheets for parallel sessions, or the main coffee area.
- **Respond to your delegates' learning preferences.** For example, some delegates like to hold a piece of paper in their hands, and use this as a map

to get from here to there. Others like 'Go along this corridor, up the stairs on your right to the 2nd floor, then turn left and it's the third room on your right.' And there are some whose earnest wish is 'Please can you just take me there. I'm late, I'm hot and tired, and I'm presenting there in ten minutes, and I need to set up.'

- **Don't underestimate how much you have learnt about the venue.** You may have been there for a day or two, or at least an hour or two more than the delegates who are just arriving. You will already have sussed out that despite all the maps referring to the Mackenzie Building, this edifice bears not a single inscription to that effect (the plaque fell off in the storm two years ago, and is still being repaired), but is the tower block to the left of the main entrance to the car park. So don't send people looking for the Mackenzie Building.

- **The delegates are always right, except when they are wrong.** It is important for you and your event team to recognize the difference and respond sensitively. Although CADS can lead to apparently disproportionate responses to difficulties the delegates are very rarely completely wrong. If they are experiencing a difficulty it means they have found something challenging you had not anticipated, or they have interpreted your information in a way you had not intended.

- **Remember that the event team can get too close to the arrangements.** Often this means the team cannot actually see details in the way delegates will experience them. When confronted by a dissatisfied delegate listen carefully, acknowledge his or her viewpoint and (be seen to) take some action. Additional signage or a housekeeping announcement will convey information to all the delegates, and show the complainer that you have taken him or her seriously, which is also part of fostering an ongoing (marketing) relationship with the individual.

- **Acknowledge when you are wrong.** In the heat of the moment, trying to do the right thing for hundreds of delegates at once, it is easy to make mistakes. Don't fudge responsibility, try to rectify the situation and learn from the mistake. (See our case study, 'Making a crisis out of a drama'.)

- **Say 'sorry' even when you are not wrong.** If a delegate has a problem, or is unhappy about something, don't concentrate on trying to work out whose fault it is. 'I'm sorry about this, what can I do to help?' is a much more productive approach, even if the problem is entirely the delegate's. CADS has to be treated with great compassion and sympathy. CADS degenerates into its chronic phase if any blame is directed at a delegate.

- **Look after your delegates.** Yes, your delegates are responsible adults, but they are at your event, subject to your timetable, catering arrangements, staff and so on, and you know that a good number of them may be suffering from CADS to some degree. You will make your life easier if you make their lives easier. Ensure refreshment and comfort breaks are at appropriate intervals, make sure dietary or medical requirements are satisfied, create an atmosphere in which delegates feel comfortable telling you if they are having difficulties. Consider including next of kin/medical information forms in the delegate handbooks for those who wish to use them.

- **Anticipate delegate needs.** Think of what you would want out of a conference or workshop experience, use feedback from previous events, canvas anecdotal opinion from potential delegates, and use information you have gathered on the booking forms. Above all cater for a wide variety of disability and accessibility needs, and assume that at least some delegates will arrive at your event with requirements they have not notified in advance.

- **When is a delegate not a delegate?** If your event is residential and targeted at a national or international audience, you may receive requests for delegates' companions to be accommodated at your conference. This is particularly the case if you have chosen a location with tourist appeal. Decide from the outset what you are and are not able or willing to do in response to such requests. You will need to establish your administrative processes for these situations, and as appropriate, know what extras you need to charge. Remember it is not just for you to make the decision. There is no point promising a double room which the venue is unable to provide.

- **'Honey, I'm nuts about you!'** Just because two people appear to be together, do not assume they are in agreement about their requirements. If one says he or she has a nut allergy, and the other denies it, check with them both to be sure. If one delegate claims to be the partner of another but they have contacted you separately, discreetly check with both what their accommodation requirements are. If your accommodation arrangements are based on strangers sharing twin rooms, do not make assumptions about their gender based on their given names. You get the picture – don't make assumptions that could be embarrassing to you or your delegates.

- **The delegate arrives with a companion; now what?** If you have a significant number of international delegates accompanied by partners who want to see the sights, you might consider arranging a spouses' programme of organized visits and outings when the delegates are busy with the pro-grammed business of the event. Unless your conference is extremely well endowed with financial and human resources this would be best outsourced to a specialist company. The icing is often the bit that goes runny and spoils a perfectly good cake. This of course is all premised on an assumption that the delegate has warned you in advance and made an appropriate booking for the companion. You will need different contingencies in place for the unexpected.

- **No, the unexpected companion cannot sleep on the delegate's floor.** Although this sounds like a harmless revisiting of a long-lost student experi-ence, there are serious implications to turning a blind eye to gatecrashers. In the event of an emergency evacuation you will need to have an accurate idea of who you are accounting for. A gatecrasher is also unlikely to be covered by either your or the venue's insurance in the event of an accident.

● **Care for the carers. Not all accompanying non-delegates are having a holiday.** You must make provision for accompanying carers. Potential delegates with specific care or support requirements may travel with an assistant who will need to be accommodated appropriately. Have a separate tariff of accommodation/catering charges so that carers are not charged as full-price delegates. Invite delegates to discuss their requirement in confidence with the conference team so you can make exactly the right arrangements. You might also consider briefing a designated member of your stewarding team about individuals with specific requirements, so they can assist the carer or the delegate. Make sure your assistance is welcomed and needed by the delegate and his or her companion. Great offence can be caused by appearing to assume dependency by those with disabilities or other specific requirements.

Conference acquired dependency syndrome – some examples

No one told me that the play on the social programme was in two halves, so I left after the interval without realizing that there was more to come. It was a shame, because the other delegates said the second half was really good and helped it all to make sense.

I think the joining instructions should have told us where we could get a newspaper.
(Delegate at an event held in a city centre university campus)

I didn't realize that I would be charged for my phone calls and the drinks I took from the mini-bar, so it was a shock when I got charged a huge amount when I checked out. I should have been told that the payphone would have been so much cheaper.

I left my bag with reception staff, and when I asked at the registration desk, no one knew anything about it.

(Delegate who had left bag at the main venue reception desk on arrival, but thought he had left it at the conference registration desk elsewhere on the campus)

I left my conference bag with all the slides I needed for my workshop on the back of my chair in the cafeteria, and when I returned to collect it, I got someone else's bag instead of my own. Our bags should have been supplied with name labels.

Food for thought

Planning the catering can feel as though it takes more time and energy than planning the rest of a conference. The following suggestions may help you to learn from other people's past triumphs – and disasters!

- **Whatever else goes right, delegates will remember the food that goes wrong.** There is something fundamental and almost primeval about delegate responses to food. It is so essential to their basic survival and the subconscious perceptions of what is important. The conscious mind may be quite content that the range and content of the programme was well planned, effective, interesting and delivered by well-informed professionals, but if the subconscious is hungry, dissatisfied or alarmed, that will be the enduring memory of the event.
- **Forewarned is forearmed.** Ask delegates about their dietary special needs several times – when they first apply to attend the event, when they register, and as a housekeeping announcement early in the event itself. If you have done everything you can to find out about special food and drink needs, and they have not responded by telling you about their particular requirements, it is then not your responsibility if the provision is not satisfactory for them (but of course still try to do what you can to meet those needs that materialize at short notice).
- **Everybody has different expectations for the food at events.** Those used to attending heavily-sponsored functions may have high expectations for the food, and be disappointed by the 'school dinners' generally offered at some large events. You cannot accommodate every delegate's likes and dislikes but you can aim for consistent quality. Whenever possible use venues or caterers that have been recommended, and sample the food at a venue before confirming your booking.
- **Think ahead to the likely climate during the event.** For example, if you are doing your reconnaissance visit in the middle of winter, snow is on the ground and a chill wind is blowing, you may not anticipate that when the event actually takes place in the middle of a heat wave in the summer, the main problem could turn out to be the need for cool water to be available in copious amounts in all parts of the venue (not least the hot rooms in which presentations and workshops will be going on).
- **Respect international delegates' body clocks.** If they have travelled some way round the globe to be at your event, they could expect (and need) food and drinks at odd times (not least in the middle of the night when everything is closed). The availability of vending machines can help to solve the problem, but also make sure that there is a way that they can get coinage to use the machines. It is also worth including in the delegate handbook directions to the nearest late-opening shops, or all-night garages, for any delegates who need to find food when there is nothing available on-site.

- **More people will complain about interesting food done badly than boring food done well.** There may be a temptation to become over-adventurous with your catering in an attempt to stand out from the crowd and avoid the ubiquitous 'quiche and curly sandwiches' event lunch. This is understandable and should be encouraged, but with the warning that people's expectations will be raised when they see a spread of unusual and interesting options, so just make sure the food is as good as it looks.
- **Be careful about the speed of catering.** For example when lunch is being laid on at a hotel venue, check out carefully how long it could take, especially if the hotel is hosting two or three different events besides yours. A one-hour lunch break may seem fine, but if lunch actually were to take an extra 15 minutes it would be really awkward, as some time-conscious delegates may skip dessert and coffee to get to the next session on time, only to end up waiting, irritably, for their by now sweetened and caffeineated colleagues to drift in before the session gets under way.
- **Avoid lunchtime queues.** Participants' enjoyment of a conference can be either made or broken by their experience at lunchtime. Avoid queues by staggering sessions, laying on sufficient serving points, or providing a long break which will also enable delegates to engage in other activities such as networking or viewing the exhibition, and spread the demand for lunch over an extended period.
- **Don't provide a buffet with its back to the wall.** Just pulling out the buffet tables so that participants can load their plates from both sides of the table can double the speed at which a large group can be fed. This makes much better use of people's time than standing in queues. Similarly, when serving tea and coffee, it can make a huge difference to have several dispensers or serving stations.
- **Provide some non-stimulating drinks.** Not everyone actually drinks tea, coffee or alcohol. Have alternatives available, at refreshment breaks, at conference meals, and at any time in the conference for delegates who may need a glass of water, a fruit juice, and so on. Do not end up with those who do not happen to drink tea, coffee and alcohol feeling they are getting second-best treatment at the event. The alternatives should be seen as no less expensive than the mainstream provision.
- **Think twice about having drinks from machines.** While it is good policy to have drinks machines available to delegates as a matter of routine (for example for between sessions), it can take ages for a large group to collect drinks, especially from those machines that serve freshly prepared coffee from cartridges, at about the rate of one cup per minute. Such machines have featured top of the complaints list from many a conference.
- **Know what you are eating.** Any departure from the 'quiche and curly sandwiches' menu nearly always involves anonymous parcels of crispy filo pastry or similar containing. . . ? Who knows? Unless each item is labelled every delegate is thrust into a reluctant voyage of discovery. Some may

appreciate this, but the vegetarian biting into a juicy prawn or chicken concoction most certainly will not, and you as event organizer would certainly prefer not to induce a medical emergency for a delegate with a peanut allergy. Insist on all food being clearly and accurately labelled, especially for finger buffets.

- **Aim for food and surroundings in perfect harmony.** Try to strike the right note during refreshment breaks and meals. If you want to provide leisurely networking opportunities during your mid-morning break, serve the coffee and biscuits in a comfortable lounge area. If you want people to eat their lunch swiftly so they can move on to a demanding afternoon of sessions without delay, serve a finger buffet with functional rather than comfortable seating. If a particular meal is the principal focus of the social programme, make sure the food is good and the setting appropriate. In short, decide on the function and ambience you want for each separate catering experience during the event, and make sure you specify the menu, surroundings and service accordingly.
- **Don't forget about packed lunches.** For example, if your event is held in good weather in an attractive climate, delegates may prefer to take a packed lunch outside with them, and relax under the trees or beside the lake. If the conference happens to end at lunchtime, many delegates will prefer to take a packed lunch with them to enjoy on their journey, rather than hang around for yet another meal in the venue itself. The costs of providing packed lunches are quite modest, if the planning is done in advance. Delegates could be invited earlier on in the conference to reserve a packed lunch if required. The costs are offset by the savings likely to result from not over-catering for the final conference meal.
- **Go for the maximum benefit for the majority of people.** Although this is a rather utilitarian view, it is a sound principle to adopt in arranging catering for an event. Avoid selecting things you know will be contentious and inspire a larger number of requests for individual solutions. For example you may wish to avoid serving pork or alcohol-based sauces, especially at large or international events. Try and define a menu that will be widely acceptable even if that means erring on the side of dull. The more complex the menu, the more special diets you will find yourself catering for. This is less of a problem in a self-serve canteen situation, where a choice of dishes is available, but it is a major consideration for a conference dinner.
- **People with dietary preferences are not just fussy.** It is absolutely essential that you meet the dietary needs of those who have advised you of their requirements, and helpful if you anticipate a few extras that have not been notified. You really do not want to deal with unnecessary medical emergencies because you have ignored an allergy or food intolerance. Remember too that a vegetarian option is not the same food with the meat removed. Vegetarian or vegan delegates who have eaten nothing but salad for three days will be rightly aggrieved if they are not offered appropriate vegetarian protein.

- **Kosher and halal are not the same as vegetarian.** You may find that some Jewish or Muslim delegates say they are vegetarian because they think it is easier for the conference team. In actual fact these and other faith-based eating regimes are far more complicated than simply avoiding pork or alcohol, and are best catered for by specialists. Factor this into your planning, and invite delegates to specify such dietary requirements when they book so you can source appropriate catering services.

- **Fish carefully.** Some vegetarians eat fish. But fish isn't everyone's taste – indeed some people have allergies to fish. If the 'meat' option is just fish, not all carnivores will be accommodated, and some will probably lean towards the vegetarian option instead. Therefore. . .

- **Have extra portions of the vegetarian options available.** It is often the case that carnivorous delegates fancy the vegetarian option when they see it, and this can lead to some vegetarians finding that their option has run out. Rather than try to police the situation, it is better to cope with this possibility by having enough of everything available to accommodate people's whims.

- **Go public with your menus.** Put printed menus on the dinner tables. Put a list of options beside the buffet table. Consider making menus known in advance, for example in the conference handbook. For many people, anticipation of food is part of the pleasure associated with it. And at least you will have the reassurance that anyone who is going to have problems with particular elements of the conference catering will have been fore-warned, and perhaps made alternative arrangements where necessary.

- **Be aware of health implications.** For example, diet-controlled diabetics need to eat small, regular meals and can become unwell if the intervals between meals are over-long. Offering only cakes and biscuits can be a problem, as these are unsuitable for diabetics who nevertheless still need to eat something. Where possible, offer fruit alternatives. It can be useful to have a small supply of suitable foodstuffs and drinks at the registration desk for those occasions when something may be needed quite urgently by a diet-controlled diabetic, for example.

- **Make yourself aware in advance where, *outside* your event, people can get food.** If they are really unhappy with what you provide, it may not be possible for you to cater for their needs on-site, and it helps if you are in a position to offer alternatives.

The vegetarians were revolting

What happened?

Everything should have gone to plan. The conference team had done the site visit to the venue, discussed menus with the catering staff, sampled the food available, asked delegates for notification of special dietary needs, checked access for mobility of impaired participants, double-checked special needs requests at reception and then relaxed.

But they knew that they were in trouble as soon as the first of four courses arrived at the Scottish themed dinner. Meat eaters were served cock'-a-'leekie soup. Vegetarians and vegans waited an uncomfortably long time and were eventually served soup that looked identical, without the chicken pieces. Requests from the veggies for assurance that no animal had died to make their soup met blank stares. The next course, haggis and turnips (neeps) looked problematic from the outset, but actually the veggies were mollified by an absolute assurance that their haggis was lentil-based.

It was at the main course that the vegetarians really rose in revolt. The Aberdeen Angus beef was brought out for the carnivores, who then waited up to 20 minutes for their veggie colleagues to be served, not knowing whether to eat or let the food go cold.

When the vegetarian alternative arrived, it was unspeakably unrecognizable and inedible. Instead of the filo pastries filled with wild mushrooms, it was an inexpressibly ugly cowpat of grains and pulses, which was so sticky it did not leave the plate when tipped by unhappy eaters at an angle of 90 degrees. It was cold, pond green and tasteless. From all around the room, voices of dissent were raised, and the mood among both veggies and non-veggies turned ugly, as all had had their meal spoilt.

What had gone wrong?

The team subsequently discovered that the veggies had complained direct to the catering staff rather than to the conference organizers about what they regarded as inadequate lunches. The chef had taken it on his own back to adapt the menu without discussion. He was in any case quite inexperienced as the head chef had left the previous week as part of a generous redundancy deal. To ameliorate the situation, the conference organizers doubled the amount of wine made available, and insisted that a cold buffet be provided for the hungry veggies. It arrived too late, and was largely ignored. The venue eventually remitted a hefty proportion of the conference costs.

The learning points

The conference organizers nowadays write into agreements that the menu of any event will not be changed without direct authorization by the home team. They stress to venues that systems must be in place to ensure that veggies and carnivores at each table are served simultaneously. They tell delegates who have complaints about the food to tell the staff at the conference desk. They also now require menus for the conference dinner to be provided at the table, showing details of veggie alternatives at each course – including desserts that do not include gelatine.

Designing your handbook, and session options

What do delegates remember after a conference, besides the catering? The content, of course. The following tips should help you to think through your planning of the finer detail of the event itself, and the design of the accompanying handbook. These suggestions include some that relate to including workshop elements in your conference; we include detailed further guidance for workshop facilitators, session presenters, and chairs towards the end of this book.

- **Put the 'handy' into handbook.** Above all else make sure your event information is useful. Think of what information you need to impart, what the delegate will want to know and what will help avoid or overcome CADS. Separate out what you have already told delegates – there is little point in repeating information about how to reach the venue in a book they receive once they have arrived.
- **When is a book not a book?** When it is a Web site, or loose leaves in a binder, or a disk, or whatever format you think does justice to the purpose. Fit for purpose is the key. Be very clear about what you want your 'handbook' to do, and make sure you choose the appropriate medium for the content, audience and information you need to convey. Your handbook may be published in different formats – a Web site accessed in advance of the event when information is still fluid, as well as a hard copy supplied at the event.
- **Form should support function.** It will be very tempting to make your handbook into a souvenir brochure, knowing that it is likely to be kept for a long time after the event and may be passed around colleagues who were unable to attend in person. This is not a bad thing but needs to be kept in perspective. If the content is not useful even the most beautifully designed handbook will be on a fast track to the bin.

- **Help your delegates to find their way around the programme easily.** Make sure the information is arranged in a way helpful to delegates, and articulates closely with the shape and content of the event. Design elements should support this usability – different coloured paper for different days, themes or strands, for example.
- **Design should not create barriers to people's easy use of the document.** The following suggestions are worth thinking about in terms of handbook design:
  - Avoid shiny paper which reflects light and makes it difficult for people with visual impairments or other difficulties to read the text.
  - Ensure good contrast between text and background.
  - Avoid background images, watermarks or patterned shading.
  - Use a clear font in a large point size.
  - Adopt wide margins and use blank space and pictures or diagrams to break up large chunks of text.
  - Use spiral or comb binding so the book can be doubled back or easily held open.
  - There are many further factors to take into account when making something accessible and usable, so you might want to take advice from a disability adviser or trial the document with volunteers.
- **Spoilt for choice.** If your event relies on delegates making decisions about which sessions to attend, you need to make sure the handbook provides enough information for them to make informed choices. Especially for large residential events, where many sessions may run in parallel, delegates will have to assimilate a lot of information before determining their own attendance at selected sessions. Make it easy for them by keeping the information for each session in a consistent format.
- **Consider indexing by keywords as well as by author.** It is time-consuming at the compilation stage but saves a lot of time in answering questions which could be avoided by adopting a self-sufficiency approach to the handbook.
- **Use a database to collect, store and sort the session information.** Enlist technical support early, so you can find existing tools which will help you manage the mass of information you are collecting, administering and presenting. You should be able to avoid re-keying information, thereby avoiding many typographical errors, and be able to use the information for many purposes from the one database source – including presenter lists, equipment requirements, timetabling, handbook entries, indices, Web pages and so on.
- **Try to design your submission form to collect all the information you will require.** This will include information about such things as presenter availability, equipment requirements, keywords, when they originally submit the proposal. It will save you from having to collect *ad hoc* information later in the process.

- **Choose your moment.** It is a tough decision whether to provide your handbook in advance or at the event. There are advantages and disadvantages in both cases. Essentially you are balancing the advantages of making the provisional information available early with that of making accurate information available later.
- **The delegates know what sessions they have chosen, but do you?** There are several reasons it is helpful to know which sessions delegates have selected. You may have limited space in workshop rooms, and need to cap numbers or move a popular session to an alternative room. The presenter may want to maintain contact with participants after the session, or the organizer may want to poll participants for specific feedback. You may decide you don't need to know about delegates' session choices, in which case make sure you have booked rooms large enough for all comers.
- **Make it clear what sorts of session are which.** For example, reinforce that the 'work' in workshops refers to participation by participants. One of the most common complaints in conferences is that some of the workshops were just papers with (and sometimes without) an opportunity for questions tacked on the end. Speak to your facilitators before the session to ensure that they have built in true interactive opportunities.
- **Ensure that each workshop session will be chaired.** Chairs are there to introduce the presenter at the start of the session, to bring it to a conclusion at the end if an overrun looks likely, and to sort out any problems that arise (such as technical problems with equipment, insufficient chairs, individuals turning up beyond the limit). Chairs for workshops (and indeed for other sessions) should be briefed beforehand. See the guidelines towards the end of this book for thoughts about briefing notes.
- **Discuss optimum numbers for workshops in advance with facilitators.** This helps you to enable interactivity at workshops, and to suit these elements to the time and space available.
- **Provide an adequate length for workshops.** The length of time allocated will depend on the intended outcomes of the session and the activity to be achieved. However 60–90 minutes is usually a suitable timescale for workshop elements. If you choose a longer duration, timetable a break and ensure plenty of refreshments are to hand.
- **Plan suitable streams.** If running a series of parallel workshop sessions, try to timetable into streams to allow individuals to attend a number of workshops of interest. It is frustrating to be at a conference where you are hugely interested in five workshops running concurrently – with no interest in any of the others run before or after.
- **Consider whether to use sign-up sheets.** If you decide that you need to know what delegates have chosen, make the decision whether to have people book specific sessions prior to arrival or sign up when at the event. Obviously the first of these options may require you to have your entire programme

finalized before you promote your event or take bookings. Be prepared to manage late changes to the timetable.

- **Consider when to provide sign-up sheets.** Signing-up sheets at an event need to give all delegates a fair chance to make their selections and be arranged so as to avoid a scrum. For large events over several days the number of sessions will mean you need lots of space for signing sheets. The space is often hard to find, so consider rolling out the sign-up sheets a day or half-day at a time.
- **Pin completed sign-up sheets to the doors of session rooms.** If you are using such sheets, this will allow delegates to double-check the choices they have made. More importantly sometimes, it will provide the session chair with valuable information about who is supposed to be at the session, and if the session turns out to be over-subscribed, who actually booked the session. It can also be useful for the session presenter or workshop facilitator to be armed with a list of those who are there, particularly if it is decided to send out further information to those who attended.
- **This year's handbook is next year's advertisement.** Notwithstanding the comments above about over-enthusiastic design, do remember that your event handbook is likely to be kept as a resource by delegates who may well have annotated it with their own notes at sessions. Make sure you design it so this is possible. Once back at base a delegate who has had a positive experience at your event will pass the handbook to colleagues who could not attend but might do so in the future. The content and format of the handbook should make everyone who sees it wish they had been there.

Administration: time and motion

'Administration' covers all sorts of things, before, during and after a conference. The following suggestions focus in on a few particular aspects of administration, and can help to improve the smooth running of your event.

- **Time waits for no one.** If you have 300 delegates arriving for an event on a particular date you cannot greet them by saying, 'Sorry, but we're not ready yet.' From the earliest planning stages of your event identify what activities need doing when. Use a time line to work out the order of preparations, allowing plenty of time for things to go wrong along the way. If you are relying on specialist colleagues for input, consult them early and factor in their availability.
- **Encourage people to book early.** This links to issues discussed in the sections of this book about marketing and promoting your event. Give plenty of time and information to help potential delegates make their decision and submit their booking.

- **Confident staff will inspire confident delegates.** Make sure all the staff who have contact with your delegates are appropriately trained or briefed. Remember that colleagues not directly associated with your event will answer telephone queries before the event, so brief them accordingly.
- **Train your team.** If you are using temporary staff to assist with administration in advance of the event or as stewards at the event, train them thoroughly. Consider producing a team handbook with contact details for technical support, local taxi companies, medical services and so on, as well as the timetable, venue plans, and maps. Make sure your temporary staff know about, and adhere to, your organization's equal opportunities policies, appropriate language and behaviour protocols, and dress code for the event.
- **Anticipate pre-conference congestion and avoid it.** It is sensible to set different deadlines for different aspects of the conference, for example for receipt of papers, close of bookings, selection of parallel sessions. When everything comes in at once, even a well-prepared administration team can end up swamped by paperwork.
- **Refereeing takes time.** The refereeing process is one of the points in the event process where the conference team is likely to be entirely dependent on external colleagues. Make sure you have allowed several weeks for reviewers to return comments. Consider sending proposals to more referees than you actually need, or having some spare referees on call (and one or two who are willing to be really quick, too) so you have a fallback position if someone becomes unable to help at short notice.
- **Consider using electronic communication to speed up the process of getting in your submissions.** Even if only some of the contributors are able to send you their contributions electronically, you can still save time with those who do so, and ask for referee's comments on their submissions by e-mail.
- **Remember that at least some potential presenters at a conference may not want to book a delegate place until they know they are presenting.** For some would-be delegates, permission to attend your conference (or at least funding to attend) could be conditional on having been accepted to do something significant at the conference – give a presentation, run a workshop, and so on. Make sure your booking and proposal submission deadlines are complementary, and take account of the refereeing time constraints.
- **Make sure delegates know they are booked on your event.** Formally confirm bookings by e-mail or letter, stating exactly when and where the event is taking place, what type of booking has been secured, any special arrangements, and indicate when the delegate can expect further information. This will save you lots of wasted time and effort answering the 'I'm not sure if I'm booked' or 'Have I got vegetarian catering?' types of enquiry.
- **Avoid any uncertainty about where and when the event is taking place.** A lot of the anxieties which result in CADS can be avoided by making your delegates feel cared for before the event. Provide clear joining instructions when you promised them, in good time to be of use.

- **Provide the essential information about directions and locations in a format that will be easy to use.** If delegates are trying to navigate through a complicated city centre one-way system with a small, poor quality photocopied map they will arrive more stressed than if you provided clear, bold maps and directions. If there is a choice of campuses, make sure they know which one they are visiting. If they need a car park permit or small change for a ticket machine, tell them this in advance.
- **Anticipate delegates' needs.** It can save you lots of time during the conference itself if you provide links from the pre-conference pages of your Web site to the venue's own Web site, to any local tourist centre Web site, and to anything else that might be useful: for example bus and train timetables, airports, hotels and so on.
- **Make sure delegates know what to do on arrival.** In the joining instructions be very clear about the location of the registration desk and what information delegates will need to bring with them. Tell them what times the desk will be available, and what to do if they arrive outside those times. For residential events tell people where they will be staying, or where to check in, and what catering facilities will be available at different times.
- **Anticipate that some delegates will arrive too early.** Even when the opening times of the registration desk are clearly advertised in advance, you are likely to have at least some people who arrive before you have set it up. Having somewhere for them to sit and relax can take the pressure off everyone, especially if it is possible to organize an additional small supply of refreshments for the early birds.
- **Plan what to do with luggage.** It can be really frustrating for delegates at residential events to carry all their belongings – and their presentation stuff – all the way to the reception desk, only to find that they have then got to carry it all back along the route they have just come to the accommodation they have been allocated. Whilst it may not be possible to avoid this, for example when keys are being issued at reception, at least have somewhere available where arriving delegates can leave their belongings safely for a while, to get a coffee, visit the toilets and so on. Similarly, plan where delegates can store their belongings safely if they have to leave their residential accommodation (for example) by 10 am on the final day of the conference, when the conference continues well into that day.
- **A gift is a gift only if you think you are not paying for it.** It is tempting, especially for large residential events, to provide elaborate delegate bags stuffed with glossy conference brochures and free gifts. If these have obviously been funded through sponsorship, delegates may be quite happy to receive such trinkets. More often delegates will assume the delegate price has been inflated to cover the costs of irrelevant trivia. In reality it is often not expensive to provide the items, but your delegates' perceptions are the important factor. Keep any gifts useful and professional. Avoid the inevitable escalation in expectations as each conference tries to better the last bag!

6 Managing the event

This short section is primarily about keeping the event on track, from registration to departure. That said, several things already addressed in our book need to be carried forward continually at the same time.

In this section, we have provided three sub-sections which naturally overlap to some extent. The relative importance to you of these sections will depend on the context of your own conference and event. The three elements of this section are devoted to helping you regarding:

- keeping things going;
- reception and registration;
- technical support.

Keeping things going

Once your delegates are signed in and into the opening session, don't imagine for a moment that your work is over. There will be all sorts of things you need to attend to, and many of them will be both important and urgent. The following suggestions cover just some of the actions you will need to be ready to take.

- **Don't just cope during your event, manage it.** It is your event, so decide what is supposed to be going on and make it happen. For example, if people are milling around outside the main plenary venue one minute before the keynote is scheduled to start, someone has not been managing that aspect of the event. Delegates should have been gently directed to take their seats for the keynote minutes ago. The key differences between managing and coping are taking decisions, and anticipating.
- **Keep people informed.** There will inevitably be changes to the programme, cancelled sessions or emergency announcements to be made, as well as routine 'housekeeping' announcements (but see below). Use the most appropriate method for the message.
- **Use housekeeping announcements sparingly.** When your delegates are gathered in a plenary session they expect pearls of wisdom from a keynote speaker or inspiring debate from a panel of experts, not mundane details

about room changes and where the coffee is being served. Aim to provide essential information on or before arrival in the printed materials, and keep additional housekeeping announcements brief and to the point. Sometimes the announcements can be made in such a way as to provide continuity and to foster the sense of occasion – 'It's my pleasure now to thank [the speaker] who will be happy to continue informal discussion over coffee, now being served in the foyer.'

- **Keep people informed in more than one way.** If important announcements have been made in a plenary session, there are very likely to be some delegates who were not there and missed them – and even more who were there in body, but still missed them. It can be useful to have an 'Announcements' board where all important (and routine) announcements are pinned up so all can see them – or remind themselves of them. Use a large font size, and be economical with words, so that the announcements can be viewed by several people at once when necessary.
- **Use prominent notice boards.** Have separate notice boards for personally addressed delegate messages and notices from the event team. This is particularly important for longer residential events. Make sure delegates know where to look for messages and notices. Consider using the registration area as an ongoing information point throughout the event.
- **Consider having an 'urgent' area on one notice board.** Make sure that nothing that is not urgent gets there, and that there are only one or two messages there at any one time.
- **Sometimes a 'Messages from delegates' board can be useful.** This can include messages from delegates to the organizing team, and turn out to be a useful ongoing feedback channel. In particular, however, it can be useful for delegates to put up messages about their own particular sessions, such as 'Handouts now available at reception for those who didn't get one in Session 24', and so on.
- **Take notices down when they are finished with.** If the session that was moved to the large room because it was much in demand is already well under way, the notice to that effect has served its purpose. If the mobile phone found in the car park has already been reclaimed by its owner, take that notice down.
- **Room and programme changes are very disruptive.** Try to avoid them, but when they are unavoidable make sure people know about them. Put notices on the doors of the original room and the replacement room, use stewards or event team staff to redirect people and post notices on the message boards. Try particularly to avoid escalating room or programme changes.
- **You can't stop things going wrong.** Just make sure you have a strategy for handling the unexpected. Have a contingency plan and revisit it during your conference preparations. Scare yourself by thinking of the worst things that could go wrong, then reassure yourself by making a judgement of how likely each occurrence is, what impact it would have on your event, and what you

would do if you had to cope with the situation. It will be much less frightening if you have anticipated what you would do in even the most unlikely circumstances.

- **Plan to be able to provide speedy technical support.** If a data projector or overhead projector suffers bulb failure for example, that particular session is in crisis, and needs rescuing quickly. It can be really useful to have mobile phone links to two or three people who can quickly get to such a problem and help out.
- **Think through how best to use sign-up sheets for parallel sessions.** These never work perfectly, however. Accept that the word will have got around that Session 32 is likely to be really good, and 43 delegates will have arrived at Room 234 which only has chairs for 24, and several delegates who were among the first to sign in for the session will arrive when all of these chairs have been taken. Wherever possible, have at least some spare chairs not far from any room which seems likely to be about to become a popular choice.
- **Re-brief and re-group.** It can be really useful to plan in short team updating meetings at two or three points during the event itself. These meetings need to be short and sweet – possibly over an extra cup of coffee. But they can be vital for keeping all team members up to date with any changes in plan which have just been agreed, or any notable occurrences which they should all be aware of, such as 'suspicious character noticed outside the exhibition area, wearing a black balaclava'.

Reception and registration

The staff who run the conference reception point, which is often the registration desk as well, are likely to be the first people to meet delegates. Such staff therefore create important first impressions of the event as a whole. The following suggestions are based on the experience of Deb Chapman, who has stood behind many a conference reception desk, and should help to make life better for many people doing this kind of work at conferences, and indeed in some of the earlier planning stages before the event.

- **Don't buy cheap badges.** Conference badges that come apart and drop off are not worth having. The time and trouble of having to supply delegates with replacement badges is something you can do without. In any case, it gives a poor impression to conference delegates if the conference seems to have been put together on the cheap – especially if it is quite an expensive conference, and some of the delegates are paying for it out of their own pockets.
- **Know when to ask for a temp.** For example, pre-prepared personalized luggage labels to tie to (or stick on to) conference packs, suitcases and so on

are much appreciated by delegates at residential events, but incredibly time-consuming to prepare. Do not allow senior colleagues to spend this sort of time themselves, even if it was their idea to have such luxuries. Persuade them to get a temp in.

- **Have sufficient staff.** Typically one person can manage to register up to around 40 delegates, but for greater numbers it can be worth bringing in further help, possibly by hiring a receptionist from an agency for the most busy registration period.
- **Wear comfortable shoes.** Choose the most comfortable you can find even if they look unattractive. You are likely to be on your feet for a lot of the day, and you could cover some miles.
- **Wear *quiet* shoes.** If, for example, you could be the one charged with the job of popping in and out of plenary sessions with the camera, and particularly if the plenary room has a wooden floor with boards with a tendency to squeak when walked upon, don't wear the kind of shoes that would cause the sound of you slipping in and out to reverberate around the room. If the speaker happens to be really boring, the sounds you may make could be the most noticed sounds in the room. And if the speaker is inspiring everyone, you will irritate them all. Similarly, if your job could extend to finding a delegate in the middle of a session to deliver an urgent message, make sure that you can move around with the minimum of noise.
- **Sit down when you get the chance.** If you are staffing the reception desk, for example, make sure there are some chairs for when the pressure is off. A suitably positioned chair or two can be useful, not least for the delegate who arrives at the registration desk tired and flustered to catch breath before moving on.
- **Don't rely on volunteers (or pressed people) to help out at peak times.** Do not allow congestion. Get each person through registration as quickly as possible. Be polite but firm. Do not allow chit-chat around the registration area when other delegates are waiting. Train up a few dedicated registration staff rather than pull staff in willy-nilly when you get busy, otherwise you have to go through the whole process of explaining to colleagues how it all works each time you bring on a new person.
- **Keep well-intentioned people out of the process.** Do not let your senior management team anywhere near the registration desk (even to welcome delegates), as it can hold up the registration process as they exchange a whole year's experience with long-lost colleagues from afar, which can interfere with your well-oiled processes for booking delegates in swiftly and efficiently.
- **Know the place backwards.** Familiarize yourself with the locations of rooms so you don't feel stupid when delegates ask you where such and such a room is between sessions. And make sure you always know the quickest way back to base for those occasions where the best thing to do is to accompany them to where they are heading.

- **Split the alphabet sensibly.** Registration lists should be alphabetical, split into four or five sections so that different registration staff can work on registration at the same time. Then they can have all the information about that person's booking: for example, which type of booking (fully residential, day delegate and so on), which social programme elements booked and which parallel workshops selected. If you have pre-labelled delegate packs already sorted out, containing the appropriate mixtures of paperwork, meal vouchers, event tickets and so on, sort them into four or five alphabetically arranged sections, and place each lot into a box so that they can be shuffled through easily and systematically when searching for a particular name. Don't stack them in a pile or a heap.
- **Take care with numbers.** Always check delegates' membership numbers, if such things are linked to your conference booking arrangements, for example in connection with members' discounts at a professional association conference. Don't rely on members to get their numbers right.
- **Think ahead too.** For example, it can be useful to ask incoming delegates whether they will require a taxi upon leaving and at what time (this facility is always appreciated).
- **Take all your own kit.** Take everything from your own office drawer – stapler and staples, adhesive tape, Blu-tack, drawing pins, scissors, rulers, erasers, pens, pencils, notepads, hole punch, sticky notes, spare pens, calculator, spare battery and all the other things you need in your normal job. You are likely to need just about all of these things sometime in your conference work – usually at short notice when it really helps not to have to scrabble around looking for such things.
- **Present a professional image.** Keep your registration area as uncluttered and well organized as possible. Design you registration area so there is adequate space for the number of delegates arriving. A frenzied crush at registration will be an unfortunate first impression for delegates, especially if they are tired after long journeys or anxious about unfamiliar surroundings.
- **Decide how many registration staff you will require.** The majority of your delegates are likely to arrive within a short period of time just before the event opens. Make sure you anticipate surges in delegate arrivals and have adequate registration staff to cope. Train them thoroughly in the registration process so you don't need to draft in extra help from colleagues who are unfamiliar with the system you have devised.
- **Make delegates feel welcome.** Be friendly to each delegate however busy the registration desk becomes. Have a checklist of essential information you need to give to, or receive from each delegate, and anticipate some of the questions you will get. 'The first session will be in room x starting in 10 minutes.' 'Dinner will be served in the refectory at 7.30 pm.' 'All the information you require is in this handbook.' 'The stewards in blue t-shirts will be able to answer your questions, and can help you with your luggage if needed.'

- **Don't forget that even experienced conference delegates may feel disoriented.** For many reasons discussed under 'delegate issues' your attendees may feel unsettled on arrival or may be tired after long journeys, so make sure you have enough trained hands to offer advice, help with luggage and direct delegates around the venue. Consider recruiting a team of stewards for larger events. Where possible, recruit stewards locally; their more detailed knowledge of the venue and its surroundings can be most helpful to delegates (and to you).

- **Provide information at registration in a convenient format.** Some information is best issued at registration – final timetable, name badges and so on – but if delegates arrive burdened with luggage they will not appreciate a handful of loose bits and pieces. Think carefully about what information and literature you are providing, and present it appropriately. Are you supplying pens, blank paper or free gifts? All this needs to be taken into account when deciding what to hand out at registration and how to present it: bound handbook, wallet folder or in a carrier bag. Consider using personalized envelopes (which can be prepared in advance) for name badges, specific messages, luggage labels, chairpersons' briefing notes, and other items of information that are specific to particular delegates.

- **Know what information to provide, and when.** There is little point in supplying a handbook in advance with the joining instructions if you have to issue a revised one at registration. Even if the pre-issued handbook is correct and accurate, the number of delegates who remember to bring the documentation with them to the event may be disappointing. Consider supplying early information through a Web site rather than in hard copy, and encourage people to familiarize themselves with the event content in advance. Whatever you decide, make your decision about when to finalize information and stick to it.

- **Don't assume that delegates will bring with them everything you intended them to bring.** This applies to pre-issued handbooks, maps, and all sorts of paperwork you may have sent out in good time for the conference. Some delegates will not have received them – they may have been on holiday and come straight to the conference. Some delegates will have lost them. Always keep a reasonable number of spare copies of anything which has been sent out, but don't place these on display at reception, or everyone will think they have to take (another) copy.

- **Plan to get your own back.** Take pre-printed labels for return of your goods when the conference has finished, and all of the paperwork and resources remaining at the venue need to be couriered back.

- **Look after your staff and help them look after themselves.** Your team will work long days at events. At a residential event, they may be on duty, to at least some extent, from waking up to retiring for the night. Make sure they know what working hours are involved in advance. Brief the staff about looking after themselves, and schedule in rest and refreshment breaks. For long events like residential conferences, consider providing a common room for stewards and staff, and maintain a ready supply of drinks and snacks. If staff have to work outdoors, advise them to be prepared with sun cream, hats, waterproofs as appropriate to the season/local weather.

● **Plan a holiday.** Take the week off after the conference if possible – you will be shattered! Knowing you have a break coming up shortly can give you that bit of extra energy and determination when the pressure is on.

When is an office not an office?

What happened?

With due concern for the stewards' welfare at a residential event, the conference team used a large teaching room as a combined office and common room. The room was the only room available not being used for workshops, and was the hub of the event operations. Two-way radios were recharged in the room, stewards and conference staff took their breaks in there, essential supplies of snacks and drinking water were stored (and consumed) in the room, office and exhibition stationery were available for use by the conference team, external phone calls came through to the 'office' – all in all, a recipe for complete chaos. Most of the time the room resembled a noisy landfill site more than an office, but it was 'home'. It felt so homely, in fact, that those stewards posted around the campus but with little to do decided to have a sing-along and make contact with their buddies at base, forgetting that anyone, delegate or staff, within earshot of one of the radios could hear it all. So it was quite unfortunate that the organization's senior managers chose it as a good place for impromptu meetings and interviews with journalists.

It did not take long for delegates to realize where the real activity of the event was happening, or where a stash of useful stationery and snacks could be acquired. Even so, most were happy to refer to the information desk and accept the advice offered about where to purchase stationery or food.

'I'll just go and find out for you,' said the steward, and headed for the conference office unaware of the delegate tracking him. Once aware of the conference lair, that particular delegate spent the rest of the conference bypassing the information desk and coming straight into the conference office, resisting all polite requests to do what everyone else did and take enquiries to the desk.

What did we learn?

Be very clear what purpose a room is serving. If you need a common room for stewards or staff, supply one, but don't think it will double as a peaceful and professional work space, let alone a senior management think-tank or media briefing room. If necessary try to secure several small rooms that can be used for distinct purposes.

Provide food and snacks for stewards and staff, but make clear your expectations regarding housekeeping and tidiness. It's very difficult to either relax or be professional in a messy environment.

Two-way radios can be invaluable for a large event over several days and on a spread-out campus, but again be very clear how they are to be used. A sing-along is light-hearted and harmless, but an unguarded comment about a challenging delegate, broadcast around the venue, could be extremely damaging.

Protect your space. The team is there entirely to make the event successful and enjoyable for the delegates, but the team works incredibly hard for very long hours during a residential event, and it is essential their non-public space is protected. If some delegates are perceived to have privileged access to the conference team, stationery supplies or whatever, others will soon follow suit and make similar demands.

Technical support

When an item of technical equipment does not work, or stops working, or is not there when it was expected to be there, even a minute can seem an eternity, especially to a presenter. The following suggestions should help you to minimize the risks associated with technical equipment.

- **Make it clear what equipment and support you are able or willing to provide.** Even very experienced presenters and workshop facilitators are understandably anxious before delivering a session. Make sure you have asked presenters at an early stage in the planning what equipment they require.
- **Clarify 'the usual, please'.** Sometimes a particular presenter may be a regular, and be tempted to short-circuit spelling out requirements by saying 'same as last year' and so on. But don't take anything for granted; check out quickly what exactly is expected this time round.
- **Discuss any unusual requirements.** If in any doubt, ask presenters exactly what they require and what they plan to do. If you are operating on a particularly tight budget or have made a decision not to have data projection facilities, make this very clear to presenters in advance, so you are managing their expectations of what you are able or willing to provide.

- **Don't make it worse for them by not having the equipment set up correctly.** Bear in mind that it is you the presenter will blame if the equipment he or she expected is not in the room and working. Allow time in the programme for equipment set up and changeovers.
- **Do it right and do it fast.** Once you have made the commitment to provide particular technical equipment, make sure it is adequately supported. Have reliable technicians to set it up, and who can respond quickly to problems during sessions. A presenter who feels let-down and abandoned to public humiliation because of technical failure will not feel positive about your organization or your event. A presenter who thinks he or she has been saved from public disgrace by rapid and sensitive technical support will sing the organizers' praise wherever he or she goes. Just think how you would feel in the same situation. If you are hiring technical equipment, try to arrange your own technical support as part of the deal, as it is unlikely the venue will want to support someone else's equipment.
- **Have plans for contingencies when things go wrong.** Encourage presenters to arrive prepared with their material on disk, and be prepared to produce slides and handouts for them in the event of technical failure. Where presenters hope to demonstrate something online you might suggest they have a downloaded version on disk in case the site is down or the link fails. Acknowledge in advance that technology can be unreliable, and do what you can to encourage presenters to come prepared.
- **The key to rapid response is communication.** Make sure your conference or event team are easily recognizable, and that they can communicate easily with the specialists within the team. Have a list of phone numbers of key support personnel, venue staff, technicians and so on. For larger events where you may be using a large venue or campus, consider the use of mobile phones or two-way radios to keep your team in communication with each other.
- **Ensure that all your equipment is securely kept.** Event venues are by their very nature open to visitors, and it is not always easy to distinguish your delegate from someone else's, or the legitimate delegate from the gatecrasher. You cannot be certain that everyone milling around your venue is there with good intent, so be vigilant and don't leave expensive equipment (or personal belongings) unattended. Make sure you are adequately covered for loss, damage and theft, and be very clear whether it is your responsibility, or that of the venue, or if you are hiring equipment, the responsibility of the hire company. Make yourself aware of the incident reporting mechanisms for all concerned, not least those of the venue, the hire company, the police, your own insurance company and so on.
- **If possible, have access to equipment kept in reserve.** You will often be spreading technical resources like data projectors quite thin, and may not have enough for every room or session. Even so, try to make sure you have some items in reserve to cover technical breakdown, or for situations where the presenter unexpectedly needs the equipment. If you are hiring equip-

ment, try to include spares in the deal to cover technical failure or unexpected need.

- **Consider whether you want to audio record or video key presentations.** If you want to make a permanent audio or video record of any sessions, make sure you have the technical capacity to do so. If you are using a large auditorium or lecture theatre, check with the venue what technical support is supplied as part of the package, or what you will be expected to pay. Be very clear whether these charges are extras charged by the hour, session or day.

- **Choose venues with appropriate facilities.** When selecting a venue you may want to check what support and facilities are available for those with sensory or auditory difficulties. Many larger venues are equipped with induction loops, listening posts, microphones and transcription facilities, but you need to check if the level of provision meets current legal requirements or your own equal opportunities policies.

Now you see it, now you don't

What happened?

The session sign-up sheets showed that the session was going to be very popular. Delegates had taken the initiative and ignored the 'session full' warning, and kept signing the sheet. The presenter, obviously flattered, was more than happy to have the session moved from the workshop room to the plenary auditorium.

Without fuss the conference team swung into action and implemented the room change procedure, carefully thought-through during a contingency planning session. Stewards were posted at the original room and the new room, notices were placed on the doors of both rooms and on the conference notice board. A couple of stragglers were taken in person by the steward posted at the original room to avoid any unnecessary delay in their finding the new room.

Almost 50 delegates were successfully directed from one room to another at opposite ends of the building with only three or four minutes of disruption. Nobody was denied access to the session, the delegates were comfortably accommodated – presenter and participants were happy.

Five minutes later the technician from the IT hire company told the conference manager that a laptop computer worth almost £2,000 had disappeared from the original room.

What did we learn?

Never leave anything unattended even for a moment!

The contingency planning is an effective tool but it does not mean you have thought of everything. Our focus on the customer – the presenter and delegates – meant the room change was flawless from their viewpoint, but costly from ours.

However thoroughly you brief your stewards, you will forget something vital. The steward who escorted the stragglers may have been very helpful, but on this occasion he might have done better to stand guard by the deserted room full of expensive equipment.

Having the right insurance meant we could be angry about the theft, but did not need to be despondent. The insurance policies may be expensive and add to the event costs, but they are still more cost-effective than having to reimburse the hire company £2,000.

7 Following up an event

Most conference or event organizers are quite exhausted by the time the last delegates depart. Sometimes it is triumphant exhaustion. Sometimes it is the exhaustion that makes you believe that you should never attempt organizing another event ever again! However, a period of mature reflection is helpful here, and giving yourself this space provides an opportunity to separate gut reaction from genuine reflection. It is the work that you do immediately after an event in terms of following up and taking things forward that makes all the difference to the way your event is perceived, by both the organizing team and those who have been delegates. In this section of our book, we offer suggestions regarding three areas in which things can be done after the event itself. Many of them can pave the way towards improving a future event. The sub-sections are:

- evaluating your event;
- disseminating the outcomes of your event;
- planning for your next event.

Evaluating your event

Once you have held your event, the natural reaction is to want to collapse in a heap and concentrate on recovering. But the work you do at this stage in finding out how well each element of the event has gone and analysing this for the future is invaluable. All too often event organizers think about evaluation at the very last minute, shove a hastily drawn-up questionnaire into the conference pack, and fail to think about what they will do with the data once they have it. This section is designed to help you think about evaluation in an orderly and systematic way.

- **Don't always assume a questionnaire is the best answer.** Sometimes asking people to write three key messages to the organizers on sticky notes, and stick them on the walls as they leave may give you as much information as you need. If you want them to reflect on their experiences a little, you might like to ask them to complete a stamped addressed postcard you provide for them to post in once they have returned home. In some cases, targeted telephone surveys may be invaluable if you want in-depth feedback.

- **Think about what kind of information will be useful to you and design a manageable means of finding this out.** Don't just ask everything you can think of. Identify a relatively small number of questions that will help you, for example, to plan future events or develop the next stage of the project, and focus primarily on finding out about these.
- **If you are using questionnaires at a large event, discuss with your IT staff how to design a machine-readable form.** Simple factors you might not have thought of, like placement of boxes on the page or shading of the sides of the boxes to make them look attractive, might interfere with their ability to be read through a scanner.
- **Don't ask too many questions.** Otherwise the delegates filling in the form are likely to get fed up half-way through the exercise of filling it in, and throw it away half-completed. Consider having a number of short questions that you want everyone to answer, with space for more detailed responses that enable people who want to give you a lot of feedback to do so.
- **Think carefully about what responses you are seeking.** For example, if you ask delegates to tell you the three best and worst things about an event, they may struggle to find three bad things to say, but will do their best to oblige, and you might end up with more negative feedback than you might otherwise have done.
- **Read the responses calmly.** Remember that the people who have been motivated to respond to you are likely to be atypical: that is, they are those who really liked the event and those who had some problems and issues with it. Those who thought the event was fine or average are less likely to commit themselves to telling you this.
- **Don't allow yourself to be too thrown by some very hostile and negative comments.** These are likely to have been written in the heat of the moment, and may be stronger than is merited by mature reflection. Sometimes the strong feeling will have been dissipated simply through the act of writing these robust comments. Also, remind yourself that just because some delegates included negative comments does not necessarily mean that they had an overall bad time at the conference.
- **Celebrate the positive comments and share them around.** Let everyone involved in organizing the event have access to the plaudits, and even consider putting them on the wall near your desk to cheer you up when you are dealing with the next glitch or trauma.
- **Provide an opportunity for respondents to give you contact information (on a voluntary basis).** Sometimes you might wish to follow up their comments by phoning or e-mailing them for clarification or advice. You often learn a great deal about negative comments by getting the fuller picture, and you may well be able to recruit those making really positive comments to help you with future publicity, reviewing conference session proposals or in other ways.

Disseminating the outcomes of your event

For most event organizers, it is important to maximize the impact of your event by attempting to capture and continue the buzz and enthusiasm of the event, and getting outputs into the public domain. Effective dissemination does not happen by chance, and needs to be as carefully planned from a very early stage as any other aspect of the event. Here are a number of key decisions you need to make in order to make the dissemination process as smooth and as effective as possible.

- **What do you want to tell people?** Do you want to disseminate all of the work presented at your event or simply selected highlights, for example the keynote speeches? Are the presentations the most important outcomes, or the notes of the discussions that followed? In some cases, where the purpose of the event has principally been networking, the key outcome is the list of attendees and their contact addresses, but of course this has important data protection implications.
- **Who do you want to tell?** Thinking about your audience is crucial to getting your message across. It is relatively easy to send out material in paper or electronic form to all the people who attended the event, but after that, what is your target audience? A small group of opinion-formers, a wider community of interest or the world at large? What access do you have to appropriate mailing lists? If you want people actually to read your material, it is always better to send it to named people rather than using a grapeshot approach.
- **What do they want to know?** Remember that there may be a big difference between what we want to tell people and what they want to know. It is important really to analyse user needs prior to attempting dissemination, and to find out how best to make material accessible and usable.
- **Do they want to continue to participate?** If so, consider providing a discussion forum facility on a post-conference Web site, and advertise its availability. As with any electronic discussion, it will require nurturing, moderating and stimulating. Once it is no longer being used, discontinue the facility promptly – an expired discussion forum of old messages is not a pretty sight.
- **What medium do you want to use?** Options include:
    - hard or softback edited collections of conference papers (self-produced or produced in conjunction with a commercial publisher);
    - edited volumes where selected authors are asked to write chapters on the event theme, based on what was presented there but shaped in the light of responses received from the audience;
    - Web pages (either containing everything or selected and edited as for a book);

- articles published in a special issue of a journal (needs early-stage negotiation with journal editors and publishers);
- articles in local or national newspapers and magazines;
- conference reports and so on.

Whichever medium you choose, you will need to balance manageability, pragmatism and budget together with the need for a prestigious and widely usable output.

- **How are you going to assure the quality of the outputs?** Some conference proceedings are simply lightly-edited collections of all the papers presented at a particular conference, and as such are both lacking in prestige and unattractive to readers (although they may assuage the vanity of presenters who all get a publication out of the experience). If material is selected according to available criteria and edited to give the collection a cohesion that stems from a shared topic and sense of values, then the outcome is likely to be highly-regarded, whether it is presented on paper or electronically. This is not likely to be a cheap option, however, in either time or money.
- **What is the best means of getting to them?** Putting absolutely everything up on the Web is tempting, but unless it is particularly well-indexed and ideally searchable, it is unlikely that it will be used well. Paper publications tend to be more expensive in terms of production, but tend to be less ephemeral and are still preferred by many.
- **How much can you afford to spend?** High quality production is expensive. You can save money, for example, by self-production, by using cheaper paper or by not using professional designers, but you will need to do a careful cost–benefit analysis to help you produce outputs that are fit for purpose and enhance the impact of your event. It may be better to go for fewer, well-presented materials than to produce larger-scale less well-regarded outputs.
- **How are you going to ship it out?** Don't forget to cost in the administration costs of taking orders, packing and mailing out paper production, and for maintaining and updating electronic resources.
- **How are you going to let people know the material exists?** With large-scale events, you may need to think about building in additional publicity costs for the dissemination of materials. With electronic materials you will need to devise a strategy to ensure that your material is linked to other related material and is publicized to your community, probably through e-mail.
- **Once you have produced material, how long will it remain current?** Information is not static, and you will need to decide on the approximate shelf life of material before you send it out to an unsuspecting world. This is particularly important with electronic resources.
- **How much are you in a hurry?** Electronic publication is attractive because it is fast, but may not be the most effective means of reaching your target audience. Publishing in book form may be very slow (time is needed for a proposal to be accepted by a publisher, then for production of the manuscript, editorial revisions, and perhaps 18 months is taken from submission of

manuscript to the book's appearance in the shops). Nevertheless, book formats are attractive to authors and many users. Journal production may be equally slow but is highly regarded by writers who may be keen to establish or maintain a publications record. A newspaper article may give you an instant hit but by tomorrow will be consigned to the bin. You have to decide what is most important for you, your contributors and your audience.

- **Electronic publication may be quick, but it is not cheap.** Although you save the hard copy print and distribution costs, material still needs proofing, designing and editing. In addition, the infrastructure for Web distribution needs to be robust, and this can be very costly. People's expectations regarding electronic publication are different, and you will need to review and maintain electronic resources in a way that is not required for static hard copy publications.

- **How important are the outcomes?** Does the material merit a press release? It might be worthwhile to telephone a specialist journalist to discuss the content of your event and to put him or her in touch with one or more of the speakers. Help the journalist by identifying a good angle or a catchy story where possible. Don't expect him or her to run a general conference write-up. Instead offer for example profiles, summaries, outlines or tasters of the most interesting parts of the event.

- **What would constitute a successful dissemination strategy for you?** Be realistic in what you are likely to be able to achieve, and plan ahead for it. It is often better to achieve a few really successful outcomes than to try to achieve wider but shallower coverage.

- **What would a failed dissemination strategy look like for you?** Brainstorm the worst contingencies (for example, no one bothers to write up their material for the Web site, no one wants to edit your book, you cannot interest a commercial publisher, or whatever) and try to plan well in advance to avoid these things happening. You can then tailor your own and your delegates' expectations.

Planning for your next event

What next event? Would any sensible person seriously consider planning yet another event hard on the heels of the last one? Yes and no! These tips suggest ways you can use your experience of a recent event to enhance the success of a subsequent one – if you can find the energy to do so.

- **Note down your impressions of the event.** Do this soon, before the conference or event becomes a blur in your memory. Consider what worked and what did not, what you have learnt, and what you would now do differently.

- **Debrief your event management team.** Ask for evaluative comments from your team, perhaps over an informal lunch. Do this as soon after the event as you can, particularly if some members of your conference team were only employed on a temporary basis, or were drawn from other roles or jobs in your own organization.
- **Debrief your planning team.** Ask for feedback from all who contributed to the planning. Try to find out from them if the plan and the reality diverged, and if so, why. Ask them how they feel that things could be changed or improved next time round. Ask them what is the most significant thing they now know about conference planning, with the benefit of hindsight.
- **Analyse evaluation data.** Try to gain a dispassionate view of the delegate perspective of the event. Think laterally about ways you can remedy areas that led to negative comments. Just as importantly, however, look carefully at areas where delegate satisfaction was most forthcoming, and look at how you can build on these aspects of your conference next time round.
- **Have a break!** Try to distance yourself from the past and future events for a while. Perhaps take some holiday, or immerse yourself in other work responsibilities, or concentrate on tangential professional activities.
- **Then start planning your next event.** Distil the cumulative feedback received from your previous event, so that you can use it effectively as a planning tool when you plan the next event. Begin the process all over again – but with several important learning curves already ascended this time. And good luck!

Wise after the event!

What happened?

When the delegate checked in at the registration desk, he explained that his companion was his daughter who was also staying in the city. He was issued with his conference bag, information pack and room key. No one objected when later his daughter was seen enjoying the welcome tea and cake provided for arriving delegates, but alarm bells should have rung when they were both observed poring over his detailed conference programme. They were quite discreet, so it was not until the second day that different members of the team noticed that she was appearing at every meal, and also popped up in the workshop sessions and plenaries alongside him. A mild challenge by the conference director was refuted absolutely. By breakfast on the last day it was apparent that the 'daughter' was taking advantage of a full conference place without payment. It seemed a bit late in the day by then to challenge them and besides, no one really knew what to say.

Learning points

- With the best will in the world, it is not possible to prevent some unscheduled visitors taking advantage of the conference organizers in the form of the odd meal taken or the occasional workshop attended by a non-paying participant, especially at a large residential event. However, asking delegates to show their name badges before meals are provided usually prevents the worst excesses of what is, in effect, theft taking place.
- Many conferences offer reduced price places for companions and spouses, where food and accommodation is charged for at cost, and some even offer a spouse programme. Asking delegates to sign up for workshops and monitoring who actually attends each may be possible, but is very difficult to put into effect absolutely.
- The course director in this case took the possibly pusillanimous view that she did not want to make a fuss in the absence of hard evidence, especially as her suspicions were not fully confirmed until the very end, when it was rather late to do anything. Probably she should have asked the delegate to leave part way through the conference, but ultimately she decided that the hassle and possible negative PR involved at this stage was not worth the effort.
- The conference team is much more vigilant nowadays about the possibility of people taking advantage.

8 Resources

Our aim in this section of the book is to get you started on briefing your presenters, chairs and workshop facilitators. Many conference or event teams provide guidance to such people in advance of the event, and the checklists and suggestions we present in this section have evolved over many years, and through countless conferences and events we have been involved with.

The advice we have provided on workshops in particular is more extensive, as this can be one of the areas of high risk at typical conferences.

Some elements of this section you may be able to use just as they are, or with a little fine-tuning to the context and scale of your own event. Alternatively, however, we hope that the checklists and advice in this section will provide you with an informed starting point from which to design your own briefing materials.

A checklist for presenters

Preparing for your presentation

- **Plan your paperwork.** Work out what you want your audience to have in their hands during the presentation (or before it). Photocopying facilities at a conference are usually limited and chargeable, so arrange to send to the venue – or better still bring with you – sufficient copies of any handouts.
- **Plan your added value.** Work out what you want your audience to take away – not just the paperwork, but excitement, inspiration, new ideas.
- **Plan your publicity.** Work out what advance information your audience should receive. Choose the title of your presentation carefully. Make it look interesting if you want a provocative audience.
- **Get copies ready.** When possible provide a printed copy for delegates to take away from your presentation, rather than giving it to them at the start of the session. This helps them to stay focused during your presentation, rather than to 'switch off' in the knowledge that it is covered in the handout. Provide sufficient copies for about half as many again as your estimate of the likely number of attendees, or arrange to mount the text of your presentation on an appropriate Web site after the event.

- **Sort out your visual aids.** Prepare some transparencies (or PowerPoint slides) to help you explain the main points you wish to discuss. Don't prepare too many, however – audiences become frustrated if bombarded with too much visual information. Make sure that it will be easy to read your slides from the back of the room. Use at least 18-point print size (or even 24 point), bold face, and easily-read fonts such as Arial (or clear hand printing on overhead transparencies).
- **Prepare your own copy.** Mark up your own copy of the paper, to map out how you are going to base your presentation on it. Make skeleton notes of the things you intend to explain and discuss.
- **Practise your timing.** Aim to 'deliver' for only about half of the total time of your slot. (However, have some additional things to say should there be silence when you ask for questions.)

Giving your presentation

- **Make an appropriate first impression.** When you start giving your presentation, your audience is busy making all sorts of assumptions about what sort of person you are. You never get a second chance to make a good first impression. It is worth planning the first minute or so with care, depending on the assumptions you wish your audience to make about you.
- **Make sure everyone can see you and hear you.** Look at your audience. Respond to the body language of your audience. Take notice of expressions of agreement and disagreement on faces. Just be yourself, don't play-act – you're not in for an Oscar.
- **State the objectives of your presentation.** Don't have more than three or so such objectives. Explain your intentions. You will not have time to tell everyone about everything in the paper you may be going to issue to them, so decide what you are going to do in the next 20 minutes or so – and tell your audience about this.
- **Don't just 'present'.** Remember, the purpose of a conference presentation is to engage the audience in discussion of the issues arising from your work – not just to present a research paper.
- **Keep to time.** That means (say) a maximum of 25 minutes in a 40-minute slot. It's dangerously easy to overrun, but if you rob the people in your audience of the chance to ask questions, they feel cheated. It is often the question-time that clarifies learning. Surprising as it may seem, most people are delighted in the event of a session finishing before it was due to finish.
- **Don't read things out to your audience.** Refer to the paper in your audience's hands by all means, but don't read bits of it out to them. It is far better to direct people to parts of your paper along the following lines: 'If you look at page 3, you'll see the results we obtained. The thing that really surprised us about these was. . .' Similarly, when using overhead transparencies, don't

read out to your audience the points they can read for themselves on the screen. Point to them but don't read them aloud, unless asked to do so.

- **Don't be afraid to pause.** There's nothing at all wrong with a little silence now and then. Your audience needs time to ponder and reflect. Don't be embarrassed to say, 'Think about this for a minute.'
- **Consider giving your audience copies of your slides directly.** For example, append copies of them to your paper (perhaps reduced to three to a page with room for notes, or six to a page). This makes it clear to your audience that you don't expect them to transcribe what they see on the screen, and prevents you from falling into the trap of taking away the images on the screen 'too soon'.
- **If you are giving copies, make them accessible.** Some delegates may find three per page or six per page handouts too small, especially if the slides include diagrams or flowcharts. Two per page might then be better. Have a set of full-size copies of slides, and a copy on disk, in case these are requested from you by delegates with visual impairments or dyslexia.
- **Consider making your slides available separately.** For example, make them available electronically, by putting them on a Web site from which they can be downloaded, or offering to e-mail them to delegates on request.
- **Come to a conclusion – don't just stop when time is up.** 'The rest of the developments are described on pages 7–10 of the paper' is far better than trying to rush through everything else you would like to have said. Then review the main points, ready to hand over for questions.
- **Make sure everyone knows what question you are answering.** Repeat people's questions so that everyone can hear them. (This should be done by the chair, but often isn't!) Repeating the gist of the question also gives you some seconds to think out your reply.
- **Keep notes of any adjustments you may wish to make to your paper.** If your paper is going to be published, and if there is time to make changes, it is often very useful to add to the paper the main points that were raised in questions and discussion. This can be done as an appendix, but in this age of word processing it is even better done by slipping in additional 'matters arising' in the body of the paper at appropriate places.

Guidelines for workshop facilitators

Workshops can be an invaluable element within conferences. They provide an opportunity for participants to do what they are there for – to participate – and for conferences to do what they are organized for: to enable participants to confer.

Sadly, though, many workshops belie the term, and presenters constantly hijack these sessions to provide an extended paper, to the dismay of those

117

present. There is far more criticism of 'poor workshops' than of 'poor papers' at conferences. One reason is that a workshop may well be scheduled to last 90 minutes, sometimes longer. If you are 'trapped' for 90 minutes or more in a situation where you are bored, patronized or irritated, you will be more critical than if you have suffered a mere 40 minutes' frustration in a 'poor paper' session. The problem is that many workshop facilitators do not see themselves as facilitators. They are in the business of giving extended presentations. If you are planning to run a workshop based on telling participants all about things you have done, think again! The essence of a good workshop is things participants do during it.

So how can you ensure that the workshops at your conference truly are workshops, and participants gain from attending them? The following guidelines will help.

What is a workshop?

A workshop is not a lecture – though it may contain some short episodes in lecture mode. A workshop is not a seminar. It is not just a discussion. A true workshop does not have an audience, it has participants. If participants are clear about the nature and purposes of your workshops, they will get more out of them – and so will you. Variety is the spice of workshops. What makes workshops different from presentations, lectures, courses, or seminars? The variety. Any good workshop is based on a mixture of processes, most of which involve participants doing things rather than hearing about them. It could be said that workshops are based on experiential learning, particularly that which occurs in groups rather than from simply sitting as part of an audience. In fact, several things distinguish a workshop from a presentation. A workshop may be a conference session where:

- each participant emerges able to do things better than he/she could at the beginning;
- each participant actively contributes for most of the time;
- participants learn a lot from each other;
- the emphasis is on process rather than content;
- there is a product, which encapsulates the ideas and experience of all the people present;
- the outcomes are dependent on the contributions of the participants rather than from input from the leader;
- the overall outcome is a learning occasion based on the experience of the participants, rather than on the knowledge of the leader.

What can you get your participants to do during your workshop?

Here are just some of the possibilities.

- Get to know each other using an 'ice-breaker'.
- Give you their expectations, telling you what exactly they hope to get out of your workshop.
- Suggest or negotiate one or two agreed ground rules for the workshop.
- Select from alternative workshop ideas, based on a short introduction from you.
- Share their experience and expertise.
- Brainstorm – generating ideas and solutions to problems.
- Explore resource materials you provide them with, or that they bring with them.
- Work in groups, on problems and issues.
- Report back with their ideas and suggestions.
- Use you as a resource in developing their ideas (and yours).
- Use you as an 'expert witness' – question you about your experience.
- Join in on a concluding or reviewing exercise, drawing together what they have got out of your workshop, and reporting this back.

Plan your workshop on the activities your participants will engage in, not on the content you might like to tell them about. Plan to make the content available to them in other ways, such as papers, handouts, exhibition materials, demonstrations, illustrations, recordings and so on. It is best to have sufficient activities to keep your participants going for twice the time available – and to select carefully the most appropriate half of these activities, depending on what your participants really want to get out of your workshop.

Publicizing your workshop

If you are planning to run a workshop, you need to make your workshop attract the most suitable delegates to participate in it, and to do this you need to provide useful, relevant information for the conference documentation. You will have noticed how careful commercial publishers can be when designing book covers so that they attract readers. The same principles apply to advance publicity for workshops. This is particularly true when your workshop is one of several on offer (for example a parallel session at a conference). Yet so many examples of advance publicity are dull, monotonous and off-putting – and then people complain that hardly anyone turned up for their workshop session.

What do intending participants want to know?

- What the workshop is about (your workshop title and rationale).
- What exactly they will get out of it (your intended outcomes),
- How it will run (your outline programme).
- Who is running it (brief biographical notes about you).

What do conference organizers need to know?

- That it will really be a workshop, and not just a long presentation.
- An indication of the sort of tasks participants will engage in.
- The sort of equipment you wish to be available.
- Your requirements regarding room layout, projectors, flip-charts and so on.
- The maximum and minimum numbers of participants you can accommodate at the workshop.
- Whether you will be prepared to repeat the workshop if participant demand is high.

Putting together your workshop flier

Your workshop flier is what normally needs to appear in the conference documentation, explaining to the right delegates why it is worth them participating in the workshop. It may explain the importance of the topic. It may highlight the particular difficulties that the workshop will address. The suggestions below are intended to help you to make the most of designing your workshop flier, not least as it will help you to sort out exactly what your workshop is intended to achieve.

First, choose a good title. It is best if titles are short and sharp. If they can be made 'punchy' or vaguely amusing, so much the better. Here are some titles. Which workshop would you choose to go to from the list below? Don't worry about the topics – feel the titles!

1. Performance indicators for the appraisal of quality in the design of training evaluation
2. Competence – competitive or collaborative?
3. An introduction to the basics of writing open learning materials
4. Computing for the terrified
5. Exploring evaluation
6. Training lecturers to stop teaching.

Here are some thoughts on those as titles.

1. Far too long. What on earth is the workshop really about? Looks heavy.
2. Nice one – it's got a bit of a ring to it.
3. Not good. Who would admit wanting to be introduced to the basics? 'I don't want to be seen to admit this.'

4. Much better. This is a nicer way of explaining that the workshop is suitable for beginners.
5. A good one – short and sharp. Also the word 'exploring' sounds attractive – it sounds participative rather than didactic.
6. This one hit the nail on the head at a higher education conference – and still attracted large numbers of participants (all hoping that the title did not really mean what it said!).

As an alternative, think of a title and subtitle. This is often a good way of having a punchy title, but giving a bit more detail without making the title itself longer. The following examples may trigger your imagination further.

- Learning styles – myth or reality?
- Assessment of prior learning – the Emperor's new clothes?
- Performance indicators – uses, abuses – and excuses!
- From competence to excellence? From 'can do' (or 'once did') to 'does brilliantly'.
- Defining quality in education – never mind the teaching, feel the learning.

Spell out your rationale

When you write this part of the advance publicity, try to sell your ideas to likely participants. Do not overdo it, though. One good paragraph should suffice – not three pages. Don't stand on your professional dignity when writing the rationale for your workshop. The important thing is that intending participants get a clear impression of what the workshop is about. Essentially, the rationale should explain why the topic of the workshop is likely to be important to the delegates who choose your session. The rationale as set out on the workshop publicity material should set the scene, but very briefly – it can be expanded upon at the start of the session if necessary. If the rationale is too long on the publicity material, the effect can be to dilute the impact of the event, or even to put people off booking up for it. In practice, it is best to compose the rationale after designing the intended learning outcomes, and after planning the rest of the workshop programme. This is because it is only after thinking through how you are going to approach running the workshop that you can make good decisions about exactly what can (and what can not) be addressed during the time at your disposal.

Setting your intended workshop outcomes

What are people going to get out of your workshop? This is the time to be specific (and optimistic). Intended learning outcomes should be:

- Specific – in other words they should spell out exactly what workshop participants will be able to do after taking part in your session.
- Measurable – participants' learning gain should not just be 'in their minds' but should be reflected in their actions after the event, in ways that can be seen and (if necessary) quantified.
- Achievable – in other words the intended learning outcomes should not be 'noble aspirations' but practicable targets, realistically possible within the timescale and scope of the workshop.
- Realistic – the intended learning outcomes should not be over-ambitious for the context and timescale of the workshop.
- Time-specified – it should be possible to specify which of the intended learning outcomes will have been achieved during the workshop itself, and which will remain to be developed as workshop participants continue to develop in their own work the learning that they take from the event.

Tips on formulating intended workshop outcomes

- **Avoid words such as 'understand' or 'know' or 'appreciate'.** Such language is too vague. Rather than specify that 'by the end of the workshop participants should understand so-and-so' it is much better to focus on what they should have become able to do with the learning they have gained during the event. In other words, people's 'understanding' can only be quantified in terms of their actions, and a good workshop should be designed to impact on participants' practice, not just their thinking or knowledge.
- **Make it clear that the outcomes relate to the participants themselves.** While it is perfectly possible to state intended outcomes as those of the event itself (for example, 'The objectives of this workshop are to explain the relevance of SENDA to computer-based learning design'), it is better practice to address the intended learning outcomes directly to the participants (for example, 'After participating in this workshop, you will be able to take into account a range of special educational needs in screen design aspects of computer-based learning').
- **Design intended learning outcomes partly on a 'need to know' basis.** For example, work out for yourself what your workshop participants are likely to need to achieve through your workshop.
- **Adjust learning outcomes to include what participants may also 'want to achieve'.** Often, the 'need to know' agenda and the 'want to learn' agenda coincide. However, there are usually additional aspects that participants want to learn, whether or not they actually need to achieve them. Wherever possible, represent both in your intended outcomes. 'Wanting' to learn something is a much more powerful driver than merely 'needing' to learn it, so it is worth doing whatever you can to ensure that at least some of your intended learning outcomes will address participants' wants and not just their needs.

- **Make the intended outcomes personal rather than remote.** For example, it is worth making the most of 'you' and 'your' in the outcomes, rather than simply stating, 'Participants will be able to. . .'.
- **Don't state too many intended learning outcomes at a time.** For a typical conference workshop, two or three such outcomes are enough. If the list of intended outcomes is too long, the programme will appear too formidable – especially if it is just a one-hour session.
- **Make sure that the intended learning outcomes are not just 'aims'.** The outcomes should be sufficiently specific that participants will be clearly aware of the extent to which they have actually achieved them by the end of the training event. With 'aims', it is usually only possible for participants to have begun to work towards them during an event, rather than have actually achieved them. Intended learning outcomes should be quite specific and self-contained.
- **Check that the intended learning outcomes do not appear trivial.** This sometimes happens as a result of well-intentioned efforts to make sure that the outcomes are specific, achievable and measurable, rather than broad or general. Each intended learning outcome should be seen as worthwhile in its own right by members of the target audience for the event.
- **Work out what you really mean by the intended outcomes.** It can be very worthwhile to look at each outcome in turn, apply the phrase, 'What it really means is. . .' then draft out two or three alternative versions of the original outcome. Very often, at least one of these alternatives will be much better than your original version.
- **Road-test your intended learning outcomes with colleagues or friends.** Ask them to tell you what they think that the intended outcomes actually boil down to in practice. This can help you to fine-tune the outcomes even further, so that they are as understandable and self-explanatory as possible to the target audience.

In short:

- Make the intended outcomes belong to the participants. For example, 'By the end of the workshop you will be able to. . .' rather than, 'At the end of the workshop participants will be able to. . .'.
- Start each intended outcome with 'sharp' active words such as 'handle', 'use', 'discuss why' and 'explain how to'.
- Keep it down to two or three intended outcomes.
- Don't use words like 'understand' – even when you mean them! Ask yourself, 'How can they show me that they understand it?' and use the words that come to mind as a result of this question.
- Don't make the intended outcomes look too much like hard work – even when they are hard work. Take the sting out. Make it seem reasonably likely that the person reading them will actually achieve them all. After all, conference workshops don't (usually!) last all day.

Drafting your workshop outline programme

Since intending participants will wish to weigh up whether your workshop will run in an interesting way, your outline programme needs to look interesting. Of course it needs to contain start and stop times, and a coffee break if it is a long workshop with a break in it. But it also needs to say a few words more than just content. See the boxed sample.

Outline Programme: (Title)   **Workshop 12: Tuesday 7 April**
Presenter: **Room J201: 0930–1130**

0930   Introduction – participants' expectations.
0950   Introductory exercise (in pairs).
1020   Plenary brainstorm: 'What's the problem with [the particular topic]?'
1030   Syndicate task on 'Prioritizing possible ways forward with [the particular topic]'.
1040   Working coffee (still in syndicates please).
1055   Syndicates report back.
1115   Workshop feedback and general discussion.
1130   Close of workshop.

To sum up: for a workshop, the advance publicity material for conference delegates should comprise:

- a well-chosen title (perhaps with explanatory sub-title where appropriate);
- a short, clear rationale or summary;
- two or three intended outcomes for participants;
- a draft outline programme.

Ideally, all of this should fit on to less than a single sheet of A4 paper – and not too crowded a sheet – for example to fit into a conference handbook. From this sheet, it should be abundantly clear to intending delegates (and to the conference organizers) that the workshop is not just a presentation or a lecture. Participants should be able to see in advance the sorts of activities they will be engaging in at the workshop, and they should also be able to see what they can expect to gain from the workshop.

When submitting a workshop proposal for a refereed event, beware of writing your description or outline overtly for the benefit of reviewers. Organizers of refereed events may ask for additional information, not intended for publication, which will be used by the reviewers. Remember that your published outline is what your participants will have used as the basis upon which they decided to participate in your workshop. If the session does not live up to their expectations they will be disappointed, especially if they think that the outline has been written cynically to get the session accepted.

Chairing a presentation: some guidelines

- Find time to meet the presenter beforehand, if you have not already met.
- Take time to plan a short but effective introduction for the presenter.
- Agree how you will, towards the end of the allotted time for the presentation, alert the presenter to the fact that time will soon be up.
- Find out whether the presenter is prepared to take questions, and if so, for approximately how long.
- Be quite insistent if time is running out.
- Have a question or two of your own ready in case there is an embarrassing silence when time for questions is reached – but don't use these questions if there is no such silence.
- Encourage the audience to respond with questions, watching for who seems most likely to be ready to make the first contribution.
- Encourage short, sharp questions; discourage 'speeches' from the audience.
- Ask each questioner to state his or her name clearly, before the question.
- Repeat (or summarize) each question, so that people in the audience who could not hear it first time have the chance to hear it again.
- Keep watching for who wants to ask the next question. Take questions in strict order.
- Avoid taking more than one question from any questioner, particularly when other members of the audience wish to ask a question.
- Give as many people as possible a chance to ask questions, not just the person in the second row who seems to have a lot to ask.
- Don't tolerate fools gladly. An obscure question wastes valuable time.
- Resist the temptation to answer the question yourself, unless no one else seems willing or able to answer it, and you really have got something important to say about it.
- When time is finally up, thank the presenter, and move the audience to 'show appreciation in the customary way'.
- As time for room changeovers is normally tight, gently persuade all present to (for example) 'Continue any informal discussions arising from the session in the foyer area or over coffee' so that the room is vacated in good time for the next presenter to set up.

Additional guidelines for chairing workshop sessions

'Chairing' a workshop is normally quite different from chairing a formal presentation. Many workshops do not really need a chair, other than perhaps to introduce the facilitator(s) at the beginning, or sometimes to coordinate a plenary discussion towards the end of the workshop. The timekeeping functions of a workshop chair remain important, but there are other useful functions a chair can adopt during a workshop, including:

- simply being an 'ordinary' participant, after introducing the facilitator;
- being an 'extra pair of hands', assisting the facilitator;
- making notes to lead to a summary of the workshop and its outcomes;
- acting as a 'normal' chair at times as and when needed;
- helping to organize participants into syndicate groups when required;
- helping to get syndicates back into plenary when required;
- keeping the facilitator informed regarding time (workshops can overrun);
- helping bring the workshop to a positive conclusion.

9 Templates

In this section of our book, we have adapted various templates to provide you with examples of some of the documentation you may think about using in connection with your own conferences or events. In several of the templates we have included a lot of administrative detail, so you can work out for yourself the level of detail you may need to use in your own documentation.

We have also included specimen formats of some of the correspondence you may need to engage in, for example when communicating with keynote speakers, paper authors – and not least those who are going to be disappointed because their paper or workshop has not been accepted for your conference.

The final template relates to something rather different. It is adapted from a checklist for a series of one-day training events, located in city centre hotels around the UK, where there is an event manager who is in charge of making sure that the event runs smoothly, but who has not been involved in the planning of the event or its content. This may give you some ideas for similar checklists you can prepare to cover your own shorter conferences or events.

Despite the detail in some of the templates, we would be the last to claim that we have thought of everything. But if you continue to develop documentation of your own along the lines illustrated in this section of the book, you will soon find out what additional elements you need to bear in mind in successive editions of your paperwork. If you come up with documentation that you think is a significant improvement on ours, we will be delighted to hear from you.

Conference session proposal form

Figure 9.1 is a detailed session proposal form for a three-day conference. It illustrates the kind of detail that can be useful if the session proposals are going to be subject to refereeing, and includes a range of other aspects where it is useful for the conference team to establish presenters' intentions and requirements.

(conference logo)   Session Proposal Form

A version of this form may be filled in online on the Conference Web site at: www.xxx.co.uk/conf. Alternatively please send your completed form to: (conference address) to arrive by (cut off date)

Section 1: Contact details

All communication regarding your proposal will be made with the person whose details are provided here. This information will not be sent to reviewers.

Title   _____

Given name(s)

Family name   _____

Employment details (please tick the relevant boxes if any of these should be included as part of the address for correspondence)

☐ Job title   _____

☐ Department   _____

☐ Institution   _____

Address   _____
    _____

Post town   _____

County   _____

Postcode   _____

Country   _____

Telephone   _____

Fax   _____

E-mail   _____

If you are affiliated to an organization other than the institution given above, and you would like this to appear on your conference name badge and in the Conference Handbook, please provide details here.

Affiliation   _____

Figure 9.1   *Sample session proposal form*

Section 2: Proposed presentation

Type of session

☐ Workshop session (90 minutes, of which 75 minutes should involve group activity)
☐ Discussion session (45 minutes, of which 20 minutes should be allowed for discussion)
☐ Poster
☐ Workshop with linked poster
☐ Discussion with linked poster

Title of proposed session/poster

Title   _____

Sub-title   _____

Presenters

Please list all presenters for the proposed session. All presenters/facilitators must attend the conference as paying delegates and will each be expected to complete a separate booking form.

Full name(s)	Affiliation (institution or organization)

Co-authors (not presenting)

Please provide a full name and affiliation (institution or organisation) for each co-author. Co-authors will be acknowledged in the Conference Handbook but are not required to attend the conference.

Full name(s)	Affiliation (institution or organization)

Session description

Please provide a description of your session (in the third person) for the Conference Handbook. This should be no longer than 150 words.

```



```

For workshop and discussion sessions:

Please describe how delegates will be actively involved during the session (up to 50 words).

```
During the session delegates will ...


```

Figure 9.1 *(Cont.)*

Please describe up to three benefits that delegates will gain from this session.

By the end of the session delegates will:

1. _____
2. _____
3. _____

Target audience

This information will be published in the Conference Handbook to help delegates choose sessions that are of particular interest to them. Unless you state otherwise it will be assumed that the session is of general interest to all colleagues. Please indicate if the session is particularly suited to individuals with a particular level of experience or from a particular subject discipline.

This session will be of particular interest to (please tick only one):

☐ experienced colleagues;
☐ those who are relatively new to the theme of the conference;
☐ delegates with a research interest in the theme of the conference.

Topic strands

Please indicate the most appropriate topic strand for this session:

☐ strand 1   ☐ strand 2   ☐ strand 3   ☐ strand 4

Keywords

A list of keywords is available from the Conference Web site at **www.xx.co.uk/conf** Please select up to five keywords from the list that apply to your session.

1. _____
2. _____
3. _____
4. _____
5. _____

You may suggest ONE additional keyword (such as a project name) for your session:

_____

Biographical notes on presenters and co-authors

Please provide a brief biographical note (in the third person) for this session (up to 50 words).

Figure 9.1   *(Cont.)*

Section 3: Planning information

Equipment requirements

Workshop sessions and discussion sessions

The following equipment will be provided as standard in all session rooms: seating for up to 30 delegates, dry wipe board or flip-chart, overhead projector and screen.

Please tick any additional requirements:

☐ No additional requirements
☐ Data projector and screen with laptop (with Microsoft Windows 2000 and Office)
☐ TV and VHS video
☐ 35mm slide projector and screen
☐ Computer lab (maximum 20 workstations)
☐ Internet connectivity (limited numbers available, so please only request if you need to have one)
☐ Other, please specify _____

Poster presentations

Please fill in this section if you would like to provide a poster, either as a stand-alone presentation or linked to a proposed workshop or discussion session. To display a poster you will still be required to attend as a delegate. A single poster board (capable of taking an A0 sized portrait-orientated poster) on which posters can be mounted using Velcro hook fasteners is provided as standard for all poster presentations.

Additional requirements (please tick if required):

☐ No additional requirements
☐ Table
☐ Single chair
☐ Two chairs
☐ Single 240v power socket
☐ Additional display space (for a second A0 sized poster)

Section 4: Data Protection Act statement

All the information you supply on this form will be stored by the Association in paper and/or electronic format for the purposes of administration of the Annual Conference. Additionally, except where stated otherwise, information supplied in Section 2 may be published in the Conference Handbook and on the conference Web site. All presenters will be required to sign a Data Protection statement when completing their booking form.

Figure 9.1   *(Cont.)*

Conference booking form

Figure 9.2 illustrates components you may wish to include in a booking form for a residential three-day conference, including a social programme, with various other elements of the form addressing special dietary needs, other special needs, and so on.

Conference Booking Form

Please send your completed form to: (conference office address)

Contact details
Membership number (if applicable) _____
Title _____
Given name(s)
Family name _____
Employment details (please tick the relevant boxes if any of these should be included as part of your address for correspondence)
□ Job title _____
□ Department _____
□ Institution _____
Address _____
_____
Post town _____
County _____
Postcode _____
Country _____
Telephone _____
Fax _____
Email _____
If you are affiliated to an organization other than the institution given above, and you would like this to appear on your conference name badge, please provide details here.
Affiliation _____

Figure 9.2 *Sample conference booking form*

Booking details

The closing date for bookings is (closing date). Bookings made after the closing date will incur an additional late booking fee of £20. Changes to booking details made after the closing date may incur a £20 administration fee. No refunds can made for cancellation after the closing date.

'Early-bird' rates refer to bookings received by (early bird date).

Member rates are available to all Fellows, Members or Associate Members.

Please tick **all** relevant boxes All accommodation is en-suite.	'Early-bird' member	'Early-bird' non-member	Member	Non-member
Whole conference residential* Includes social programme and Conference Dinner	☐	☐	☐	☐
Whole conference non-residential* Includes social programme and Conference Dinner	☐	☐	☐	☐
One day part conference residential				
Wednesday only Includes lunch and dinner and social programme on Wednesday and breakfast on Thursday	☐	☐	☐	☐
Thursday (arriving Wednesday) Includes dinner and social programme on Wednesday, breakfast and lunch on Thursday	☐	☐	☐	☐
Thursday (leaving Friday) Includes lunch and Conference Dinner on Thursday and breakfast on Friday	☐	☐	☐	☐
Friday Includes Conference Dinner on Thursday, breakfast and lunch on Friday*	☐	☐	☐	☐
One day part conference non-residential Includes lunch but does not include social programme or Conference Dinner				
Wednesday	☐	☐	☐	☐
Thursday	☐	☐	☐	☐
Friday	☐	☐	☐	☐
Additional overnight accommodation @ £xx per night Dinner not included. Includes breakfast	Tuesday ☐		Friday ☐	

*Please tick if you would prefer your Friday lunch to be provided as a packed lunch ☐

If you wish to share accommodation with someone else who is attending the conference, please provide details:

Figure 9.2   *(Cont.)*

Further details

Social programme

Please tick your preferred option for the Wednesday evening social programme:

☐ Musical recital   ☐ Ghosthunter trail   ☐ Open-top bus tour

☐ Literary pub tour   ☐ Salsa dancing

Individual needs

We are committed to meeting the dietary, mobility, sensory and other requirements of our delegates so that there is equality of opportunity for all, and the conference is enjoyable and productive. Please inform us of your individual requirements when booking (by ticking the relevant boxes and providing details) so that we can make appropriate arrangements in advance of your arrival.

Dietary requirements

☐	Non-vegetarian	☐	Vegetarian	☐	Vegan
☐	Wheat allergy	☐	Nut allergy	☐	Diabetic
☐	Other (please provide details)				

_____

Other requirements

Please tick the appropriate box(es) and provide details for any other special requirements that we should know about:

☐ None   ☐ Mobility   ☐ Sensory   ☐ Other

Details _____

A member of the conference planning team will be happy to discuss your requirements in confidence. Please tick here ☐ if you would like someone to contact you.

Figure 9.2   *(Cont.)*

Payment information

We need to receive payment for the full amount of your chosen options before your bookings can be confirmed. Payment can be made by cheque, authorised purchase order or credit/debit card. Please add an additional £2.50 administration fee if paying by credit card (ie Mastercard, Visa Credit card or JCB card).

☐ I have included a cheque/postal order (made payable to the Association) for the total sum of £_____

☐ I have attached an authorized purchase order form for £_____

☐ Please charge my credit/debit card for the total sum of £_____

 ☐ Mastercard ☐ Visa ☐ Switch ☐ Solo ☐ JCB card

 My credit card number is: ☐☐☐☐ ☐☐☐☐ ☐☐☐☐ ☐☐☐☐ ☐☐☐☐

 Expiry date: ____/____

 Issue no. (Switch only): ☐☐

 Signature _____

Data Protection Act statement

The information supplied on this booking form will be stored in paper and electronic format for the purposes of administration of the conference. Delegates' names, affiliation and e-mail addresses will be included on the Conference Delegate List unless you indicate otherwise.

For presenters, name, affiliation and biographical notes provided on the Session Proposal Form will be included in the Conference Handbook and on the Web site.

I have read and understood the above statement:

Signed _____ Date _____

☐ Tick here if you do not wish to be included on the Conference Delegate List

☐ Tick here if you are hoping to present a session or poster at the conference

Please send your completed form to: (conference office address) .

For further details contact the conference planning team on 0207 xxxxxxx, e-mail: conference@xxx.co.uk or visit the Web site at www.xxx.co.uk/conf

Figure 9.2 *(Cont.)*

Exhibitor's booking form

The pro-forma in Figure 9.3 is based on a booking form for a large residential conference, where there was a commercial exhibition.

Exhibition Packages

Commercial exhibition stand
Includes: 2m² floor space, basic exhibition shell, 1 table, 2 chairs, a 13 amp socket.
Tea, coffee and lunch for up to 2 people from Wednesday–Friday: £500.00

Commercial exhibition stand + inserts in delegates' packs
Includes: 2m² floor space, basic exhibition shell, 1 table, 2 chairs, a 13 amp socket.
Tea, coffee and lunch for up to 2 people from Wednesday–Friday.
Plus insertion of flier (maximum size A4) into all conference delegates' packs*.
£700.00

Commercial exhibition stand + advertisement in Conference Handbook
Includes: 2m² floor space, basic exhibition shell, 1 table, 2 chairs, a 13 amp socket.
Tea, coffee and lunch for up to 2 people from Wednesday–Friday.
Plus an advertisement in the Conference Handbook (please tick size required)
☐ Full A4 page (180 mm d x 255 mm w)   £575.00
☐ Half page (125 mm d x 180 mm w)   £550.00
☐ Quarter page (125 mm d x 85 mm w)   £525.00

Inserts in delegates' packs
Insertion of flier (maximum size A4) into all conference delegates' packs*
£300.00

Advertisement in Conference Handbook
☐ Full A4 page (180 mm d x 255 mm w)   £100.00
☐ Half page (125 mm d x 180 mm w)   £60.00
☐ Quarter page (125 mm d x 85 mm w)   £30.00

*Please note that all inserts must be received not later than (cut off date). All artwork for advertisements must be in camera-ready form (as a bromide or high quality laser print) or on disc (PC compatible) as a greyscale EPS or TIFF image (minimum 300 dpi). The deadline for the receipt of copy is (copy deadline). Typesetting can be carried out by the Association but will be subject to an additional charge: please contact the conference planning team to discuss details.
Contact details
Name
Organization
Address

Tel
Fax
E-mail
Names of individuals attending the conference (for name badges)
1. _____

2. _____

Figure 9.3 *Sample exhibitor's booking form*

If you wish information about your organization to be included in the Conference Handbook, please supply text of up to 150 words:

Payment and invoice details

All payments must be received in advance and can be made by cheque, authorized purchase order or credit/debit card. **Please add an additional £2.50 administration fee if paying by credit card** (ie Mastercard, Visa Credit card or JCB card).

☐ I have included a cheque/postal order (made payable to the Association) for the total sum of £____

☐ I have attached an authorized purchase order form for £____

☐ Please charge my credit/debit card for the total sum of £_____   + £2.50 if paying by credit card

    ☐ Mastercard   ☐ Visa   ☐ Switch   ☐ Solo   ☐ JCB card

    My credit card number is: ☐☐ ☐☐ ☐☐ ☐☐ ☐☐ ☐☐ ☐☐ ☐☐ ☐☐ ☐☐ ☐☐ ☐☐ ☐☐

    Expiry date: ____/____

    Issue no. (Switch only): ☐☐

Signature _____

☐ Please tick here if the package you have chosen forms part of a sponsorship agreement (details of which will be confirmed in a separate letter of agreement)

Please send your completed form to: **(conference address)**

Data Protection Act statement

The information supplied on this booking form will be stored in paper and electronic format for the purposes of administration of the Annual Conference.

I have read and understood the above statement:

Signed _____ Date _____

Terms

Please inform us of any additional requirements (for example extra tables or chairs). These may incur additional charges. Please phone for details.

None of the conference exhibitors' packages includes overnight accommodation. Overnight accommodation at the venue can be booked for an additional sum of £xx per person per night (bed and breakfast).

Additional attendees will be charged as 'non-delegate companions'. Please phone for details. The Association's Data Protection statement does not allow us to supply commercial exhibitors with a delegate list.

Bookings must be made by (cut off date). **No refunds will be made** for bookings cancelled after (last cancellation date).

Figure 9.3   *(Cont.)*

Invitation to conference keynote presenter

The letter framework in Figure 9.4 illustrates the kind of approach that may be used as a starting point, when inviting keynote speakers to a large international conference. It can be suitably scaled down for smaller events.

Address
Date

Dear (named person)

Title and date of conference

Having been familiar with your published work for a number of years and heard you speak powerfully and effectively on a number of occasions, I am approaching you to ask whether you would be available to do a keynote at our conference on the topic of (subject) on (date) at (place).

Our theme for the conference is (theme), and I wondered whether you would be interested in proposing a title of your own choice within this broad area. My first thoughts were that you might like to speak on the topic of (propose a topic based on the person's known field of expertise), but you might like to suggest an alternative title for consideration.

You can see the provisional information on the conference on the conference Web site at (Web address) for more detail of the event.

In recognition of your contribution, I can offer you a free residential delegate place at the conference, including accommodation, plus an honorarium of (fee), as well as paying for receipted standard class travel expenses.

Ideally we would like your keynote to be (specify actual time and day within the conference) but this is open to negotiation if your availability is limited. If you are able to participate in the whole conference, we would be delighted and I am sure you will find it productive and enjoyable, but we would fully understand if you could only attend on the date of your own presentation.

Other speakers confirmed to date are (other names if available, to let the speaker know what other topics are likely to be discussed at the event).

I am keen to get the publicity for the conference under way in the next few days, so your provisional response on this matter within five working days would be really welcome. If you are able to accept this invitation, a colleague from the conference organizing team will be in touch once I have heard from you, to confirm your keynote title and a brief biography and photo for the conference publicity material.

I very much hope you will be able to work with us and look forward to hearing from you.

Yours sincerely

(Name)
(Designation)
(Organization)

Figure 9.4   *Sample invitation to conference keynote presenter*

Letter to prospective authors

The sample letter in Figure 9.5, to conference presenters who may wish their contributions to be considered for publication in an edited collection arising out of the conference, could be sent to them direct before the conference, or could be included in the conference pack.

Address
Date

Dear (named conference presenter),
We are planning to publish an edited collection on the topic of the conference, 'Title of conference'. This volume will not comprise conference proceedings, in that we will expect our editors to commission chapters around the theme, rather than just collect together papers and workshop outcomes from the conference. Writers with specialist knowledge and experience in the area from the UK and internationally will be invited to contribute, whether they have attended this conference or not.

We have already had a number of expressions of interest from some conference presenters interested in contributing chapters to this volume, and I am keen to encourage further conference delegates to consider contributing a chapter also, which will broadly follow the conference themes in its structure. I anticipate that the book will ultimately comprise around 16–20 chapters of perhaps 3,000 to 5,000 words each. We will contact potential authors for chapter outlines within one month of the conference, and the deadline for the receipt of draft articles is likely to be six weeks later.

If you are interested in being considered for inclusion, please let me know, either by completing the form below and handing it in at the conference desk, or by writing or e-mailing me after the conference.

I am also interested in receiving expressions of interest from colleagues (ideally someone who has written or edited a book previously) to undertake the role of co-editor of the volume. A small honorarium will be paid for this task.

Name
E-mail
Address for correspondence
Phone number   Fax number
Interested in contributing a chapter? Yes/No
Topic area/title of proposed chapter:
Interested in being a co-editor of the volume? Yes/No
Experience of writing/editing:
You may, if you wish, attach a cv/list of your existing publications

---

Figure 9.5   *Sample letter to prospective authors*

Session reviewer guidelines

The form in Figure 9.6 can be used as a basis for designing guidelines for those reviewing proposed conference presentations or workshops.

Thank you for agreeing to review session proposals submitted for the conference.

In considering your response to the session proposals sent to you, please consider the extent to which the proposed session will articulate with the conference theme.

In the context of these themes please score each session proposal against all of the following criteria:

	Yes, extremely	Yes, reasonably	Not particularly	Not at all
Does the proposal suggest a workshop or discussion session likely to be of interest and value to conference delegates?				
Additional comments:				
In your opinion, is the session soundly based on relevant and up to date thinking?				
Additional comments:				
Is the topic current without being hackneyed or over-exposed?				
Additional comments:				
Does the methodology outlined in the proposal seem likely to involve participants fully for at least half the session?				
Additional comments:				

Figure 9.6 *Sample session reviewer guidelines*

Rejection letter

The format in Figure 9.7 can be used as a basis for drafting rejection letters to those whose proposals for conference elements were not accepted on this occasion.

Address
Date

Dear (unsuccessful proposal author)
Thank you for submitting your proposal (title) to present a conference workshop or discussion at the conference this year. I regret to inform you that we have not been able to accept your proposal on this occasion. We received more than twice as many proposals of a very high standard for this event as we could accept. Each proposal was sent to three reviewers who assessed them anonymously on a scale of 1–4 against the following criteria:

* Is the session likely to be of interest and value to conference delegates?
* Do you think the session is soundly based on relevant and up to date thinking?
* Is the topic current without being hackneyed or over-exposed?
* Is the methodology likely to involve participants fully for at least half of the session?

We then aggregated scores and also selected topics for balance and coverage. Where colleagues submitted two or more proposals we could not accept more than one. In addition, where colleagues are taking part in an invited symposium or keynote we felt that, in fairness to other colleagues also submitting excellent proposals, we could not, on this occasion, offer a second opportunity to be a lead presenter at this conference.
    I am sure you will be disappointed to receive this news. I would assure you that the process of selection was undertaken fairly and rigorously. We do hope that you will, nevertheless, join us at the conference and will submit proposals for future events.
    I look forward to seeing you on future occasions at our events.
With very best wishes

(Chair, Conference Planning Team)

Figure 9.7   *Sample rejection letter*

Medical details form

You may wish to include a confidential medical form within the event documentation (perhaps in the Conference Handbook) for delegates to complete if they have a special need they think it would be helpful for the organizers to know about. A sample is given in Figure 9.8.

Confidential Medical Form

Completion of this form is entirely optional.

If you wish to provide us with emergency medical and contact information then please complete this form and return it to the Conference Office.

Full name:

Emergency Contact

Please provide us with details of someone we should contact in the case of an emergency.

Contact's name:

Relationship to delegate:

Daytime telephone number:

Evening telephone number:

Medical history

Are you currently taking treatment for any medical condition?

☐ Yes   ☐ No

If yes, please provide details

Do you have any known drug or food allergies?

☐ Yes   ☐ No

If yes, please provide details

Is there any other medical information you feel we should be aware of?

☐ Yes   ☐ No

If yes, please provide details

Doctor's details

Please provide your doctor's details

Doctor's name:

Telephone number:

The above information is true to the best of my knowledge

Signed: _____   Date: ___/___/___

Figure 9.8   *Sample confidential medical form*

Conference evaluation form

Figure 9.9 illustrates the kind of feedback form that can be used at a large conference, to gather delegate comments about the conference itself, and various other aspects of their experience of the conference.

Conference Evaluation Form

Please use this form to provide us with feedback on your experience of the conference. This will help us in our planning of future conferences.

1. Please rate each keynote on its relevance to your work and the quality of the presentation.

	Relevance				Presentation			
	Not relevant	⇔		Highly relevant	Poor	⇔		Excellent
	0	1	2	3	0	1	2	3
Opening plenary discussion	☐	☐	☐	☐	☐	☐	☐	☐
Keynote presentation (name speaker)	☐	☐	☐	☐	☐	☐	☐	☐
Closing plenary discussion	☐	☐	☐	☐	☐	☐	☐	☐

If you have further comments on the keynotes please include them here.

2. Please comment briefly on the sessions you attended.

Session no.	Brief session title	Brief comment	Did the session meet your expectations?	
			Yes	No
			☐	☐
			☐	☐
			☐	☐
			☐	☐
			☐	☐
			☐	☐
			☐	☐
			☐	☐

If you have any general comments on the sessions please include them here.

Figure 9.9 *Sample conference evaluation form*

3. Please rate the following aspects of the conference.

		poor	fair	good	excellent
Session information on the Web site		☐	☐	☐	☐
Administration:	Pre-conference	☐	☐	☐	☐
	During the conference	☐	☐	☐	☐
Conference handbook:	Ease of use	☐	☐	☐	☐
	Content	☐	☐	☐	☐
Social programme		☐	☐	☐	☐
Conference venue:	Service	☐	☐	☐	☐
	Accommodation	☐	☐	☐	☐
	Catering	☐	☐	☐	☐
Conference dinner:	Venue	☐	☐	☐	☐
	Service	☐	☐	☐	☐
	Catering	☐	☐	☐	☐
Overall value for money ☐		☐	☐	☐	☐

Comments (use this space to elaborate on any of the above):

The following questions are designed to tell us more about your expectations from other equivalent conferences.

4. Which other conferences have you attended during this year and how did they compare with this one?

5. What type of venue would you prefer for a residential conference?

☐ University site with on-site accommodation and catering arranged by conference organizers

☐ University site with delegates responsible for arranging own accommodation and catering

☐ Dedicated conference centre with onsite accommodation and catering arranged by conference organizers

☐ Conference centre with delegates responsible for arranging own accommodation and catering

6. Do you prefer to have an organised social programme?

☐ Yes – what sort of activity would you like to see included?

☐ No

7. What items would you expect to be included in a conference package (for example conference bag, pen, notepaper)?

8. If you have come to the conference as a presenter, what resources do you expect all presenters to be provided with (eg flip-charts, board markers)?

Figure 9.9 *(Cont.)*

144

9. Finally, please complete the following two sentences:

> *a) The one thing which would have most improved my experience of the conference is ...*

> *b) For me, the best thing about the conference was...*

We may wish to follow up some of the feedback we receive. If you are happy for us to do this please include your name, institution and e-mail address below.

Full name ....

Institution ....

E-mail ....

Thank you for completing this form. Your comments will be very helpful in planning future events.

Figure 9.9   *(Cont.)*

Certificate of attendance

Some delegates may find it useful if you provide a certificate of attendance for their Continuous Professional development records or performance review meetings, or in order to claim back the conference fee from their employers. Figure 9.10 gives an example.

Event manager's checklist

The checklist in Figure 9.11 has been adapted from one used for one-day training events, where a professional event manager organizes various details of the events, which are normally held in city-centre hotel venues, and oversees that the delegates, presenters or facilitators are welcomed, fed and supported throughout the day.

```
┌─────────────────────────────────────────────────────────────────┐
│                                                                   │
│              Certificate of Attendance                            │
│                                                                   │
│  (Please take this certificate to the Conference Reception desk   │
│  if you require to have it stamped and signed.)                   │
│                                                                   │
│                                                                   │
│                    This is to certify that                        │
│                                                                   │
│           ........................................(full name)     │
│                                                                   │
│                            from                                   │
│                                                                   │
│           ........................................(organization)  │
│                                                                   │
│                       attended the                                │
│                                                                   │
│               (name of conference plus dates)                     │
│                                                                   │
│                                                                   │
│           Signed on behalf of (name of event organizer)           │
│                                                                   │
│                                                                   │
│                                                                   │
│                    ........................                       │
│                                                                   │
│                                                                   │
│         Date                    Stamp or seal of event organizer  │
│                                                                   │
└─────────────────────────────────────────────────────────────────┘
```

Figure 9.10 *Sample certificate of attendance*

Item	Description	Done/comments
1	Locate the boxes containing delegate packs if they have been couriered to the venue. Ensure that these are taken to the reception area outside the conference room by 0830.	
2	Using the company arrow signs provided in the Event Manager's folder, make sure that the conference room can be found easily from the hotel reception area or main entrance.	
3	Place 'keep this seat free' cards from the Event Manager's folder on (for example) two or three seats near the entrance to the conference room, so that latecomers can slip in easily to seats near the entrance if necessary.	
4	Meet the hotel banqueting manager or representative, and check through the details relating to the particular event, including how to get in touch with him/her if necessary.	
5	Check that the room is set out in the appropriate layout for the particular event being run.	
6	Check that there are spare chairs in the room, for group or syndicate work.	
7	Check that the room is adequately heated or ventilated. Find out where the controls for heating/ventilation are, and how to adjust these.	
8	Check that the equipment which has been ordered for the event is present in the room, and set up correctly, and working properly, including for example: • overhead projector • screen • data projector • flip-chart • marker pens. Obtain a contact name and telephone number to use if anything breaks down.	
9	Delegates' tables: check that the following are in place: • cordials and water • drinking glasses • pads and pens or pencils • name cards.	

Figure 9.11 *Sample event manager's checklist*

10	Find out the location of toilet facilities, including provision for any delegates who may be disabled.	
11	Find out the location of public telephones.	
12	**Fire drills and evacuation procedures** • Check that no hotel fire drills are planned for the day, or if one is planned find out the time, and advise chairs or presenters when this will be. • Check fire drill procedures, and find out emergency routes out of the conference room.	
13	**Lunch** • Find out exactly what the lunch options will be, and where the seating for this will be. • Remind the venue catering staff if necessary that there must be a hot vegetarian option. • Find out whether the catering staff need to know in advance how many delegates will take up the vegetarian option. • Check that any special dietary requirements have been accommodated (see Event Manager's folder for details of requirements that have been notified).	
14	**Liaison with chairs/presenters/speakers** • Welcome chairs/presenters/speakers, and invite them to stay for lunch, if not already expecting to stay. • Check that their numbers are duly included in the total number to have lunch. • Share any relevant information which they will need to know. • Give them delegate packs and name badges. • If there is a chair, introduce him/her to any other speakers or presenters. • Arrange with whoever will be leading the event up till lunchtime about a five-minute signal, so that he or she can round the session off punctually.	
15	**Registration desk** • Set this up, with delegate badges lined up alphabetically. • Either have delegate packs available to issue them at the desk, or place them ready on tables. • As delegates arrive, ask them to sign the registration form. • Direct them to where tea/coffee is being served, and where coats can be hung up. • Direct them regarding the location of toilet facilities. • Ensure that tea/coffee facilities do not run out. • Gently usher the delegates into the conference room for a prompt start, and introduce the presenter or chair, after making any necessary housekeeping announcements, including advice about valuables such as credit cards, diaries, and mobile phones. Remind any delegates who may have stayed at the hotel overnight when they will need to have vacated their rooms to avoid incurring extra charges. • When all of the delegates have arrived, confirm numbers for lunch with the catering staff.	
16	**Throughout the day** • Tidy the reception area. • Be on hand to sort out any queries, emergencies, messages for delegates, photocopying needed by presenters and so on. • Meet any further speakers arriving during the day, offer them a drink unless it is almost a refreshment break, and ask them if they want to sit in on the event until their turn comes up. • Ensure that the refreshments for tea/coffee breaks are punctual and sufficient. • Give the pre-lunch presenter the agreed five-minute signal before lunch is due. • Lead the delegates to the restaurant area. Remember to go backwards and forwards along the route for any who may have 'strayed' to telephones, toilets, and so on. • Check that the conference room is duly locked if necessary.	
17	**At the end of the event** • Collect in any badges that are offered to you. • Collect in evaluation forms, and put them in the folder ready to return to the organizers. • Check that any hired-in equipment is either collected from the conference room, or stored safely. • Take down signage.	

Figure 9.11   *(Cont.)*

147

Index

Printed in the United Kingdom
by Lightning Source UK Ltd.
131413UK00001B/281/A